Oxford
Secondary
English

Dimensions

Book 1

John Seely
Frank Green
Graham Nutbrown

Oxford University Press   1988

Oxford University Press, Walton Street, Oxford OX2 6DP

Oxford New York Toronto
Delhi Bombay Calcutta Madras Karachi
Petaling Jaya Singapore Hong Kong Tokyo
Nairobi Dar es Salaam Cape Town
Melbourne Auckland

and associated companies in
Beirut Berlin Ibadan Nicosia

Oxford is a trade mark of Oxford University Press

© Oxford University Press 1988
First published 1988

ISBN 0 19 833168 1

Typeset by Graphicraft Typesetters Ltd. HK
Printed in Hong Kong

Contents

Talking about school

Questions

Look at the drawings and read the words.

1   What do you think of each of the people speaking?
2   Why?
3   If you were asked the question, what would you say?
4   Copy this drawing and fill in the bubbles:

Writing: the details

To help you remember all the details about your last school, here is a list of things to write down:

1. The name of the school.
2. The road the school was in.
3. The district, town, or village where it was.
4. The name of the headteacher.
5. How many teachers there were.
6. How many classes there were.
7. How many children from that school are in your class now.
8. The names of all the subjects you did.
9. The subjects you liked best.
10. The games you played.
11. Your last teacher.
12. The best things you did in your last year.

Writing: what you thought of it

Make two lists. At the top of one write: 'What I liked about my last school'. At the top of the other write: 'What I disliked about my last school.'

What was your last school like?

1. The name of my last school was Great and Little Preston Junior Mixed School.
2. The school was in Preston Lane.
3. It was in Allerton Bywater.
4. The Headteacher was called Mr Charlston.
5. There were seven teachers.
6. There were four classes.
7. There is one person from that school in my class now.
8. I did Games, Swimming, P.E., Art, Maths, Writing, Singing, Topic and English.
9. I liked Swimming, Art, Games and P.E.
10. I played Draughts, Chess, Snakes and Ladders, Football, Rounders, Tabo, Bulldog, Chainies, Cricket, Stoolball and Stuck in the Mud.
11. My last teacher was called Mr Jackson.
12. The best things I did were take part in plays, go on trips and baking.

What I liked about my last school.	What I disliked about my last school.
Coming home at 3.30	Maths
Art	Topic
Games	Writing
PE	Singing
Plays	Assembly
Trip to Jorvik Viking Centre at York	
Trip to Headingley Water Treatment Works	
Playtimes	
My friends	

THORNBURY HIGH SCHOOL

The unofficial guide for first years.

Things you need to know but nobody ever tells you.

Explaining school

On your first day at your new school, you were given a lot of information, so that you knew where to go and what to do. There were probably other things that you needed to know but were not told. At Thornbury High School they have produced their own **unofficial** guide for new first years. Now you're going to do the same.

WHERE TO FIND IT
Important places in the School

1   Make a list of five places in the school that you think are important and that new pupils need to know about.
2   For each one explain:
      What it is.
      Why it is important.
      How to find it.

WHO THEY ARE
Important people you should know about

1   Make a list of five people in the school who you think are important and who new pupils need to know about.

2   For each one explain:
      Who s/he is.
      Why s/he is important.
      When or why you are likely to meet them.

WHEN IT HAPPENS
Important times in the day
Important moments in the week

1   Think about an ordinary day. Make a list of times that you think are important and that new pupils ought to know about.
2   For each one explain:
      What happens.
      Why it is important.
      Any other useful information.

FIVE IMPORTANT QUESTIONS
People always ask

Read what you have written so far. What other information do new first years need?

1   Make up five questions they might ask to get that information.
2   For each question write a clear and detailed answer.

How would you explain your school to a Martian?

Writing

Suppose you met an alien from another planet. To your surprise it speaks English.

It speaks to you and asks you to explain what a school is. Unfortunately it doesn't know the meaning of any of these words:

class	book
classroom	test
teacher	English
lesson	Maths

1 Explain each of the words so that the alien can understand.
2 Use the words to help you explain what a school is.

The new boy

The door swung inward. I stood and breathed
The new-school atmosphere.
The smell of polish and disinfectant,
And the flavour of my own fear.

I followed into the cloakroom; the walls
Rang to the shattering noise
Of boys who barged and boys who banged;
Boys and still more boys!

A boot flew by me. Its angry owner
Pursued with force and yell;
Somewhere a man snapped orders; somewhere
There clanged a warning bell.

And there I hung with my new schoolmates;
They pushing and shoving me; I
Unknown, unwanted, pinned to the wall;
On the verge of ready-to-cry.

Then from the doorway a boy called out:
'Hey, you over there! You're new!
Don't just stand there propping the wall up!
I'll look after you!'

I turned; I timidly raised my eyes;
He stood and grinned meanwhile;
And my fear died, and my lips answered
Smile for his smile.

He showed me the basins, the rows of pegs;
He hung my cap at the end;
He led me away to my new classroom . . .
And now that boy's my friend.

John Walsh

Questions

1 What were the boy's first impressions of
his new school?
2 The new boy felt 'On the verge of ready-
to-cry'. What does this mean?
3 Why did he feel like that?

4 What happened to change things?
5 How do you think he felt as he walked to
the classroom?
6 How long ago do you think this was
written? What makes you think that?

First day at school

The morning came, without any warning, when my sisters
surrounded me, wrapped me in scarves, tied up my bootlaces,
thrust a cap on my head, and stuffed a baked potato in my pocket.

'What's this?' I said.

'You're starting school today.'

'I ain't. I'm stopping 'ome.'

'Now, come on, Loll. You're a big boy now.'

'I ain't.'

'You are.'

'Boo-hoo.'

They picked me up bodily, kicking and bawling, and carried me
up the road.

*   *   *   *   *

I spent that first day picking holes in paper, then went home in a
smouldering temper.

'What's the matter, Loll? Didn't he like it at school, then?'

'They never gave me the present!'

'Present? What present?'

'They said they'd give me a present.'

'Well, now, I'm sure they didn't.'

'They did! They said: "You're Laurie Lee, ain't you? Well, you
just sit there for the present." I sat there all day but I never got it. I
ain't going back there again!'

Laurie Lee *Cider with Rosie*

Writing

a) *Preparation*

Think back to your first day at your new
school. Remember what happened.

1   Write down all the things you remember
    seeing.
2   Write down the sounds and smells you
    remember.
3   Write down any other physical feelings
    you had.

4   How did you feel — happy? sad?
    frightened? a mixture? Think of the best
    words to describe this and write them
    down.
5   Have you missed out any important
    memories? If so, write them down.

b) *Writing*

Now write a description of being a 'New boy'
or 'New girl'. Use the ideas you have written
down but add any new ones that you think of.

9

Meeting the Martian

Remember the Martian who visited your school on page 7? Since then he's been around the town giving all the local people quite a surprise.

Everybody is talking about the new visitor to the town.

July

5 Tuesday
It started as an ordinary day. I went to work as usual, but when

Alien causes traffic chaos

AS people began their way home from work this evening and the evening rush hour began to build up

What to do

Preparation

1 Choose one of the pictures on page 10.
2 Think about what happened:
   What the Martian did.
   How people reacted.
   What happened in the end.
3 Imagine that you were one of the people there. Decide what your thoughts and feelings were about it. (Did you find it funny, frightening, or what?)

4 Now look at the top of this page. Choose one of these three ways of reporting what happened:
   diary
   radio news interview
   newspaper

Writing

Tell the story of what happened, as a newspaper report, a diary extract, or a radio interview.

Favourite things

Suppose you have to go away from home for a few weeks to stay with a relative or a friend. You may want to take a few of your favourite things. Which do you choose?

Make a list of **six** things you would choose. Next to each choice, write a few words to explain **why** you have chosen it. You can include pets.

My favourite things

If I had to go away from home for a few weeks I would take:

1 My radio cassette recorder - so that I can play my favourite tapes.

2 My teddy - because I have had it since I was a baby and still like to keep it in my bedroom.

3 My photographic album - because it has lots of photos of friends and of places I've been to on holiday.

4 My chess set - because it is quite valuable and my grandad gave it to me. He had it when he was young.

5 My project on American Indians - because I did it in my old school and really enjoyed doing it. It was the best thing we did.

6 My shoes - because they are new and because I would need them.

A class survey

In this survey you are going to find out what favourite things other people in your class chose. Then you are going to make a bar chart to illustrate their choices.

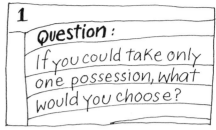

1   Write down the question(s) you are going to ask each person.
    Suggestion: only ask them which **one** favourite thing they would take.
    Otherwise your survey will get too big and complicated.

2   Ask each person the same question.

3   Write down each person's name and answer.

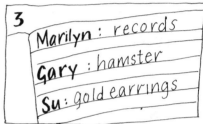

4   When you have asked everybody, sort out the answers. Divide them into groups and count the number in each group.

5   Now draw the bar chart. This is easier if you use squared paper.

More class surveys

You can use this survey method to find out other things about your class. Follow the same pattern and do a survey on one of these:
favourite records
favourite comics and magazines
favourite animals
favourite TV programmes
favourite sports and games
favourite pop stars

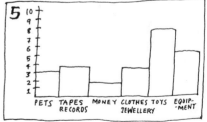

13

Explaining charts

This is a **pie chart.** Can you think why it has that name? The chart shows how often 24 children change their socks.

Writing

Write seven sentences explaining what the chart means. For example, '1. Three children change their socks every day.'

Drawing a pie chart

Either
Use the information below to draw a pie chart.

Or
Do your own survey of favourite sweets and draw a pie chart from it.

A change of socks

Every two days

Every day

Do not wear socks

Every birthday

About twice a week

Every fortnight

Every week

9 said they liked PEPPICHOC best

6 said they liked HOLO best

4 said they liked FRUITY LUMPS best

2 said they liked BALLOON GUM best

2 said they liked MOON BARS best

1 said she liked SLICKIES best

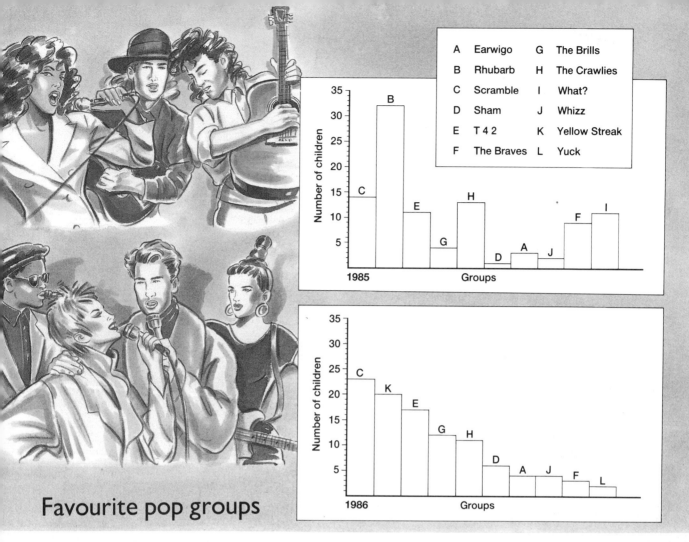

A	Earwigo	G	The Brills
B	Rhubarb	H	The Crawlies
C	Scramble	I	What?
D	Sham	J	Whizz
E	T 4 2	K	Yellow Streak
F	The Braves	L	Yuck

Favourite pop groups

A number of children were asked to name their favourite pop group in 1985. The same children were asked again in 1986. The results are shown above in two **bar charts**.

Questions

Answer these questions about the **bar charts**.

1   How many children took part in the survey?
2   In 1985 which was the most popular group?
3   In 1985 which was the least popular group?
4   In 1986 which was the most popular group?
5   In 1986 which was the least popular group?
6   Which groups are not in the 1985 list?
7   a) Which groups are not in the 1986 list?
    b) Why is this, do you think?

Writing

Write at least five sentences based on your answers to the questions.

Your own survey

Do your own survey of pop groups and draw a bar chart to illustrate it.

15

Presents

You have £6. You want to buy presents for each of these people. What would you buy and why?

Gran

Gran is 76 and lives a long way from you. You don't see her very often, but you get on really well with her. She is still very active and enjoys cooking and looking after her small garden. Her eyes are not so good any more, but she still enjoys watching TV.

Sister Suzy

Suzy is 10. She likes active things and is already quite good at games at school (rounders and athletics). She is also very interested in making things: last Christmas she was given a Technical Lego set, and she spends a lot of time making models with that.

Brother David

David is 15. He is keen on pop music, football and likes to dress well. He doesn't like reading much, except for books about flying — his one ambition is to join the RAF or become an airline pilot.

Talking points

1 How did your choices compare with those made by other people?
2 If someone very rich was going to buy **you** a present and they asked you what you would like, what would you say?
3 What is the **worst** present anyone has ever given you?
4 A close friend gives you a really awful present. What do you do:
   a) Tell your friend you don't want it?
   b) Tell the friend how much you like it, and then throw it away?
   c) Say 'Thank you' and then give it to someone else?
   d) Say 'Thank you' and try very hard to like it?
   e) Do you do something else?

Thoughts of a soldier

Once I was the treasure of treasures,
Holding the plastic gun in all sorts of poses.
My uniform was always spotless.
Arguments flared over who should play war with me.
But as time passed neglect gnawed at me.
Gone is my novelty, and my boots.
And felt tips are scrawled on my face.
I was used as a missile for throwing at people.
My arms were torn from my body.
My army cap lost.
I am now nothing but an eye-sore
With a mud-encrusted uniform from playing outside.
They didn't care a bit for me.
They don't know I even exist in this dark cellar
Sitting in sawdust all broken to pieces.
Once nobody could touch me,
Not even a fly's fragile wing.
Now though rats freely chew at my plastic body.
Once I was recognised as a fearless soldier.
Now I'm a warped bundle of plastic,
With a mud plastered uniform.
These dingy cellars entomb my distorted body,
And my lonely fears.

Writing

Preparation

Somewhere at home you probably have toys
or games that you don't play with any more,
but which used to be favourites when you
were younger. Think about these questions:

1   Where are they now?
2   Are they lying forgotten somewhere?
3   What condition are they in?

Choose one of these toys. Imagine it can think
and talk. Write down its thoughts about
happy times in the past and its thoughts about
your neglecting it.

Writing a poem

Use your ideas to write a poem. You don't
have to make it rhyme: just put each new idea
on a new line. You could start with this line:

Once I was the treasure of treasures . . .

Writing poems: First lines and last lines

One way of building up a poem is to have the same first line and
last line to each verse.

Possessions

My favourite possession
Was an old woollen blanket —
I used to chew the corner.
But then I lost it.

My favourite possession
Was a Mickey Mouse telephone —
I used to phone up the Prime Minister.
But then I lost it.

Fears

One thing I fear
Is my Mum's temper
The sort when she storms and stamps
And calls me names:
That scares me!

One thing I fear
Is the cobwebby cupboard
Under the stairs.
I know it's daft, but
That scares me!

Writing a poem

1 Choose *either* a **First Line** *or* a **Last Line**.
Make up a poem that repeats the line you
have chosen.

2 Now try writing a poem that includes
both a **First Line** *and* a **Last Line**

First lines

One thing I hate is ...
I saw a funny thing today...
I just don't think it's fair...
In my dream last night I was...
The most amazing fact I know...
In a hundred years from now...
I told a terrible lie. I said...

Last lines

People say I must be mad!
Mum says: Better luck next time!
But what can I do about it?
But no one will believe me.
You'd better believe me!
Well, that's what I think, anyway!
It may come true one day!

The playground poem

That's my football, give it back!
Trudi, done your homework yet?
Miss, Miss, my skirt's been ripped!
Quick, before the bell goes. Quick!

What's that, Penny? Let's have a look.
I saw a UFO last night.
Sure! Look over there — a fight!
Quick before the bell goes. Quick!

My Mum will kill me if she finds out.
Swap you that for this, all right?
Break it up boys. Who started it?
Quick before the bell goes. Quick!

This is just a list of things you might overhear in a playground. They have been chosen and written down in an order that makes them interesting.

Writing

Write a similar poem with one of these titles:
    The football-match poem
    The school-dinner poem
    The school-dinner-queue poem
    The netball-lesson poem
    The going-on-holiday poem
    The walking-home-after-school poem
    The lesson-without-a-teacher poem

Sort it out!

A pretty young lady called Splatt
Was mistaken one day for a cat
By a man called Van Damm
Who made pets into jam —
And now she's spread out rather flat.

Sort out the limericks

The rest of the limericks on this page have got
rather mixed up. See if you can sort them out.
There are four complete limericks. They begin
like this:

i.e.   A kindly old fellow called Clore

_____
_____
_____
_____

A young man from Redcar, called Vince

_____
_____
_____
_____

There once was a fellow called West

_____
_____
_____
_____

A lady from near Milton Keynes

_____
_____
_____
_____

Here are the jumbled lines:

1   And getting both legs through his vest.

2   Would find its way out

3   Gave all that he had to the poor;

4   It's my birthday today

5   So he's not giving them any more.

6   Had trouble digesting her greens.

7   They would not give it back,

8   And I'm right out of After Eight Mints.'

9   He used to quite dread

10   The odd Brussels sprout

11   Putting socks on his head

12   But the greens that bought screams were French beans.

13   But, alas and alack,

14   Like, 'Oh dear, I *say*!

15   Who found it quite hard to get dressed.

16   Used to drop very obvious hints

Odd man out

Find the face which is different from the others in every detail.

Crossword

Across

1   *Now*, that's what I call a *gift*!   (7)
4   Insect   (3)
6   The word missing from this sentence: 'A lot of teachers say that you shouldn't use _ _ _ too often when you write . . . I think they're right.'   (3)
7   If your car breaks down they will help you, but only if you belong.   (3)
8   When the 2 Down shines: opposite of night.   (3)
10   He had some thoughts in this Unit.   (7)

Down

1   If I get a one across, this is what it does to me.   (7)
2   See 8 Across   (3)
3   See 9 Down   (7)
4   What you have to do in this sum:
     17354958
      354810 +
     _____ (3)
5   If at first you don't succeed, _ _ _, _ _ _, _ _ _ again!   (3)
9   If you need help at school you should ask a 3 Down to come to your _ _ _.   (3)

Christmas presents

Christmas was coming.

The little log house was almost buried in snow. Great drifts were banked against the walls and windows, and in the morning when Pa opened the door, there was a wall of snow as high as Laura's head. Pa took the shovel and shovelled it away, and then he shovelled a path to the barn, where the horses and cows were snug and warm in their stalls.

The days were clear and bright. Laura and Mary stood on chairs by the window and looked out across the glittering snow at the glittering trees. Snow was piled all along their bare, dark branches, and it sparkled in the sunshine. Icicles hung from the eves of the house to the snow-banks, great icicles as large at the top as Laura's arm. They were like glass and full of sharp lights.

Pa's breath hung in the air like smoke, when he came along the path from the barn. He breathed it out in clouds and it froze in white frost on his moustache and beard.

When he came in, stamping the snow from his boots, and caught Laura up in a bear's hug against his cold, big coat, his moustache was beaded with little drops of melting frost.

Every night he was busy, working on a large piece of board and two small pieces. He whittled them with his knife, he rubbed them with sandpaper and with the palm of his hand, until when Laura touched them they felt soft and smooth as silk.

Then with his sharp jack-knife he worked at them, cutting the edges of the large one into little peaks and towers, with a large star curved on the very tallest point. He cut little holes through the wood. He cut the holes in shapes of windows, and little stars, and crescent moons, and circles. All around them he carved tiny leaves, and flowers, and birds.

One of the little boards he shaped in a lovely curve, and around its edges he carved leaves and flowers and stars, and through it he cut crescent moons and curlicues.

Around the edges of the smallest board he carved a tiny flowering vine.

He made the tiniest shavings, cutting very slowly and carefully, making whatever he thought would be pretty.

At last he had the pieces finished and one night he fitted them together. When this was done, the large piece was a beautifully carved back for a smooth little shelf across its middle. The large star was at the top of it. The curved piece supported the shelf underneath, and it was carved beautifully, too. And the little vine ran around the edge of this shelf.

Pa had made this bracket for a Christmas present for Ma. He hung it carefully against the log wall between the windows, and Ma stood her little china woman on the shelf.

The little china woman had a china bonnet on her head, and china curls hung against her china neck. Her china dress was laced across in front, and she wore a pale pink china apron and little gilt china shoes. She was beautiful, standing on the shelf with flowers and leaves and birds and moons carved all around her, and the large star at the very top.

Ma was very busy all day long, cooking good things for Christmas. She baked salt-rising bread and rye'n'Injun bread, and Swedish crackers and a huge pan of beans, with salt pork and molasses. She baked vinegar pies and dried-apple pies, and filled a big jar with cookies, and she let Laura and Mary lick the cake spoon.

One morning she boiled molasses and sugar together until they made a thick syrup, and Pa brought in two pans of clean, white snow from outdoors. Laura and Mary each had a pan, and Pa and Ma showed them how to pour the dark syrup in little streams on to the snow.

They made circles, and curlicues, and squiggledy things, and these hardened at once and were candy. Laura and Mary might eat one piece each, but the rest was saved for Christmas Day.

Laura Ingalls Wilder *Little House in the Big Woods*

Questions

1 Describe the place where the family lived.
2 What was the weather like?
3 What exactly was Pa making? (You can explain what it looked like using words, or by drawing a picture of it.)
4 What was it for?
5 What did the children make in preparation for Christmas?
6 How did their Christmas differ from Christmases today?
7 Would you like to spend a Christmas as they did? What would be its good points and its bad points?
8 Maybe your family doesn't celebrate Christmas. You may celebrate the New Year, Eid (if you are Muslim), Diwali (if you are Hindu or Sikh) — or some other festival. Describe how your family and friends celebrate.

Man's best friend

Some unusual dogs

a) The Lhasa Apso

A small dog, growing to about ten inches high. Long wavy hair which has a centre parting and comes down in front of the eyes. Needs regular grooming. Coat: honey, gold, black, or grey. A good housedog, likes children. Enjoys long walks but does not need a lot of exercise.

b) Affenpinscher

Name means 'monkey terrier' (a good description!). About 11 inches tall, with a short rough coat. Longer hair on face; has beard and moustache. Not fussy about exercise. Affectionate; doesn't like to be left alone.

c) Papillon

Toy dog, growing to about 8 inches tall. Name means 'butterfly', because the ears look like butterfly wings. Very friendly and suited to small house or flat.

d) Basset Hound

Short (only 14 inches at shoulder) but very heavy. Short-haired. Looks like a very big dachshund ('sausage dog'). Outdoor dog; needs a lot of exercise. Really a country dog.

e) Pyrenean Mountain Dog

Very large indeed. Quite long hair; affectionate expression. A good guard dog and an excellent family dog. Not a 'one-man' dog. Needs plenty of space and lots of exercise.

f) Hungarian Puli

Grows to about 17 inches tall. Unusual long coat that forms cords, like dreadlocks. Doesn't need a lot of grooming. You groom it using your fingers. An active dog. Does not demand an immense amount of exercise. A good family dog.

If you were buying a dog, which of the six dogs would you choose and why? Would you rather choose another breed of dog? If so, which one and why?

Mrs Williams

Mrs Williams wants to buy a dog for her family. They want a dog who will be a friend for all the family. They have quite a large garden but they live in a town. As a result it isn't easy to give a dog a lot of exercise.

Mrs Hargreaves

Mr and Mrs Hargreaves and their two children live in the country. They have plenty of money and they want to buy a big dog which they can take on walks, because all the family are great walkers.

Miss Birkitt

Miss Birkitt lives in a flat near the centre of Leicester. It's only a small flat and she is looking for a dog who will be a companion to her. She is out all day and the dog would have to be left alone for quite long periods. She hasn't got time to take it for long walks.

Mrs Handley

She lives on her own in a cottage in the country. She likes going for long walks and wants a good-sized dog that she can take with her. It must be a short-haired dog, because she hasn't got a lot of time to groom it.

Sorting them out

1 Can you work out which dog is which?
2 Can you work out which person is which?
3 Which dog should each of these people buy? Read the descriptions carefully and decide which dog would be most suitable for each and why?
4 There are two dogs left. What kind of person would each of these suit and why?

People

Uncle Podger

1 You never saw such a commotion in all your life, as when my Uncle Podger decided to do a job.

What are we going to do with this?

2 *Leave it to me!*

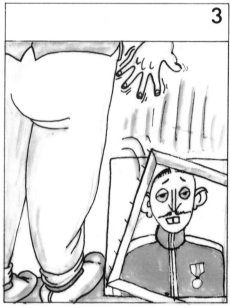

3

4

?

5 Half an hour later...

6 And then...

!---*!*

Filling in the blanks

Every picture except number 1 has a blank in it: either a *caption*, or a *balloon*.

1 Work out what should go in each blank.
2 Write down the number of each picture and the words that are missing from it.

What happened in between?

There is a gap between pictures 4 and 5. There is another gap between pictures 7 and 8. What do you think happened in each of these gaps? Make up the story of what happened in them.

What kind of person is Uncle Podger?

This is a list of words that can be used to describe people. Choose the words that are best to describe Uncle Podger. Write them down.

careful	experienced	clumsy
skilful	anxious	careless
awkward	intelligent	stupid
willing	enthusiastic	expert

Can you think of any other words to describe him? If so write them down.

Write three or four sentences describing Uncle Podger. Use the words you have written down.

Opinions about Uncle Podger

Uncle Podger thinks he's rather good at jobs about the house. Does Aunt Podger agree? Write two sentences about Uncle Podger as a handyman:

1 Said by Uncle Podger.
2 Said by Aunt Podger.

Stories about Uncle Podger

Make up a story about Uncle Podger trying to do something else. Think of your own subject, or choose one of these:
Uncle Podger goes boating.
Uncle Podger learns to drive.
Uncle Podger puts up a greenhouse.

MISSING

POLICE were yesterday trying to solve the mystery disappearance of this young woman.

A senior police spokesman said they had no clues where she might be. She left home as normal yesterday morning for the short walk to work, but never arrived.

The police need your help. Your friend is missing from home and the police have asked you to fill in a form like the one below.

Observing and describing

Copy out this form. Choose a friend in your class. Fill in the details for the person you have chosen.

Remembering and describing

It is not too hard to give details of someone who is sitting near you. It is more difficult to fill in the form when the person you are writing about is not there.

Copy out the form again.
This time choose a grown-up. Choose someone you know well. Fill in the details for the person you have chosen.

MISSING PERSON

Surname _____

Other names _____

Address _____

_____

Age _____ Height _____ Weight _____

Colour of Skin _____

Colour of Hair _____

Colour of Eyes _____

Special features (Spectacles, Scars)

_____

Other Information_____

_____

_____

28

Wanted for questioning

The police wish to interview the following man:

Arthur George Watson, a.k.a. Phil Brown, a.k.a. Lenny Ralston

Watson is 32 years of age, tall (well above average height) and thin. He has long fair hair and very pale skin. He has a moustache. He has a long scar on his right cheek. Because of an accident as a child his right shoulder is higher than his left.

THIS MAN IS DANGEROUS.
If you see him, do not approach him, but inform the police.

Who is right?

A number of people think they have seen Watson. For each of the six sightings say whether the man in the picture:

a) Definitely **is** Watson.

b) Definitely **is not** Watson.

c) **Might be** Watson, but it is impossible to be certain.

In each case, give your reasons.

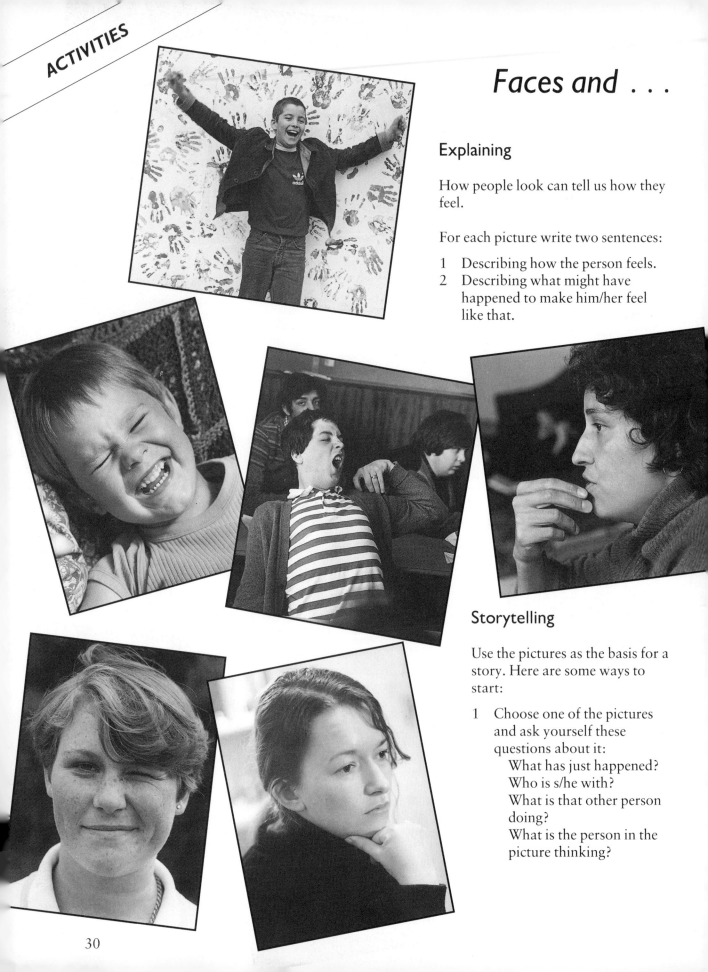

Faces and . . .

Explaining

How people look can tell us how they feel.

For each picture write two sentences:

1 Describing how the person feels.
2 Describing what might have happened to make him/her feel like that.

Storytelling

Use the pictures as the basis for a story. Here are some ways to start:

1 Choose one of the pictures and ask yourself these questions about it:
   What has just happened?
   Who is s/he with?
   What is that other person doing?
   What is the person in the picture thinking?

. . . gestures

Explaining

What people do can tell us how they feel.

For each picture write two sentences:

1 Explaining what the sign means.
2 Describing what might have happened to make the person feel like that.

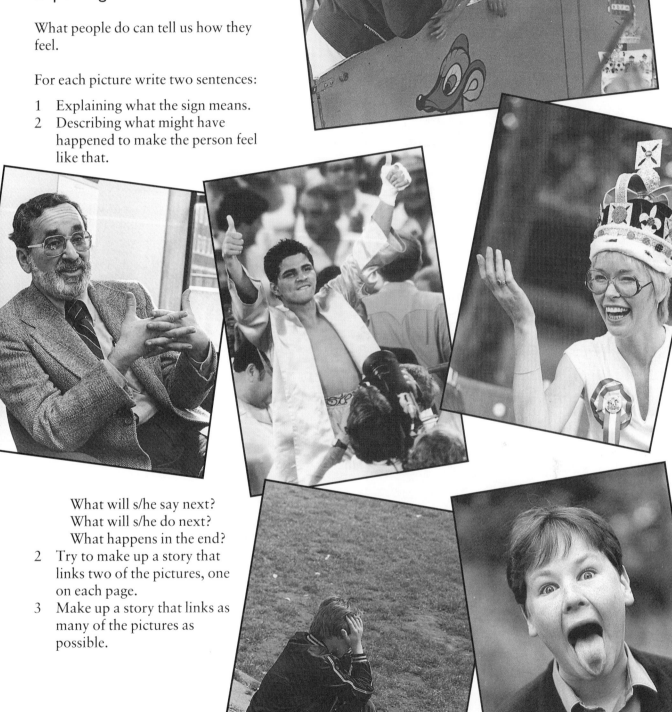

What will s/he say next?
What will s/he do next?
What happens in the end?
2 Try to make up a story that links two of the pictures, one on each page.
3 Make up a story that links as many of the pictures as possible.

Told any good stories today?

'We saw a police chase on the motorway and we heard afterwards...'

'Mum was in a bad mood yesterday evening, she wouldn't let me...'

'I've been and left my project at home; she said...'

'And then he had the cheek to say...'

'and she hadn't taken in her milk, so the postman...'

Questions

1 Have you heard any stories today?
2 Have you read any stories today?
3 Have you told any stories today?
4 How many different kinds of story are shown on this page?
5 Can you think of any other kinds of story?
6 What's the difference between **telling** and **writing** a story?

32

'...and then Tuesday, no it was Wednesday, because...'

'I've always had a soft spot for cockroaches...'

'...but it was all right because I had a bit of chewing gum in my pocket...'

'...a nice bit of fresh fish for my dinner...'

Telling stories

1 Choose one of the pictures.
2 Work out what the rest of the story might be.
3 Tell the story to a friend.
4 Now write it down.
5 Compare the two versions (the spoken one and the written one). Which is better, and why?
6 Make up other stories based on other pictures.

'The hamster got out last night and chewed up the cable of Dad's...'

Poems about people

Shed in space

My Grandad Lewis
On my mother's side
Had two ambitions.
One was to take first prize
For shallots at the village show
And the second
Was to be a space commander.
Every Tuesday
After I'd got their messages,
He'd lead me with a wink
To his garden shed
And there, amongst the linseed
And the sacks of peat and horse manure
He'd light his pipe
And settle in his deck chair.
His old eyes on the blue and distant
That no one else could see,
He'd ask,
'Are we A OK for lift off?'
Gripping the handles of the lawnmower
I'd reply:
'A OK.'
And then
Facing the workbench,
In front of shelves of paint and creosote
And racks of glistening chisels
He'd talk to Mission Control.
'Five-Four-Three-Two-One-Zero —
We have lift off.
This is Grandad Lewis talking,
Do you read me?
Britain's first space shed
Is rising majestically into orbit
From its launch pad
In the allotments
In Lakey Lane.'

And so we'd fly,
Through timeless afternoons
Till tea time came,
Amongst the planets
And mysterious suns,
While the world
Receded like a dream:
Grandad never won
That prize for shallots,
But as the captain
Of an intergalactic shed
There was no one to touch him.

Gareth Owen

34

Grandad

*Grandad's dead
And I'm sorry about that*

He'd a huge black overcoat.
He felt proud of it.
You could have hidden
A football crowd in it.
Far too big —
It was a lousy fit
But Grandad didn't
Mind a bit.
He wore it all winter
With a squashed black hat.

*Now he's dead
And I'm sorry about that*

He'd got twelve stories.
I'd heard every one of them
Hundreds of times
But that was the fun of them:
You knew what was coming
So you could join in.
He'd got big hands
And brown, grooved skin
And when he laughed
It knocked you flat.

*Now he's dead
And I'm sorry about that*

Kit Wright

Questions

Shed in space

1   Study the poem and find all the things it
tells you about the shed and what is in it.
Think of some more things that *might* be
in it. How could all these things be used
in their space game?

2   What would be the best place in *your*
home for an imaginative game like this?
3   What are Grandad Lewis's main
interests and pastimes?
4   What sort of person is he?
5   How would you describe the child's
relationship with him?
6   How does it compare with how you get
on with *your* grandparents?

Grandad

7   This is about a grandfather who has
died, but is it a *sad* poem?
8   What words would you use to describe
it?
9   What sort of person was Grandad?
10 The poem uses exaggerations. Find
them. What is the point of them?

Both poems

11 Are there any similarities between the
two Grandads?
12 Are there differences?

Jacqueline

In the first part of this story some words have been missed out. The missing words are listed underneath. Work out which word goes in which space.

The other children were ____1____ of Jacqueline.
    Jacqueline was a big girl for her age, ____2____ than all the boys, and she didn't mind barging and ____3____ and sometimes pinching in a really sore way — to get a good ____4____ in the dinner line, or bag a desk by the window, or grab the newest, ____5____ netball.
    Jacqueline told ____6____. 'Miss, Jason keeps taking my felt ____7____,' or, 'Sir, Morris and Rashid were fighting at playtime.' Sometimes she even told ____8____. 'Miss, Emma pulled my hair,' when in ____9____ Emma would never dare touch Jacqueline's hair for ____10____ of what she might do to her later.

Missing words: tips   pushing   lies   place   scared   bigger   fact   bounciest   tales   fear

In the next part of the story some more words have been missed out. This time there are no words to help you. Try to work out the best word to go in each space.

Jacqueline boasted. 'I've got ____11____ own television in my bedroom,' or 'I'm ____12____ to get a new bicycle — it costs £150!' The other children didn't really ____13____ her, but they were never quite sure. They ____14____ see, from her neat little calculator and all the sweets in her ____15____ and the films she said she'd seen that she got most things she ____16____.
    Jacqueline knew how to ____17____ people's feelings. She asked Hing Ling why her eyes were all funny. She ____18____ when Juan couldn't say a new English word. She said Darren must be a ____19____ pig to be so fat. She said Thomas's father couldn't ____20____ him or he wouldn't have gone away.

In the last part of the story, some whole sentences have been missed out. They are listed at the end. Work out which sentence goes in each space.

____1____ Perhaps that was the worst part, and no one knew how to deal with her. ____2____ Everyone tried not to notice that Jacqueline always did harder projects than the rest of them. Everyone stared stonily when Jacqueline had to show the PE class how to climb a rope. ____3____
    Except swimming.

Missing sentences:
Everyone sat very quiet when Jacqueline's drawings, poems, and stories were pinned on the wall.
She seemed best at everything.
Jacqueline was clever.

Adapted from *Shivers* by **Jane Ferguson**

Midas and the golden wish

Midas, King of Phrygia, owned everything a man could wish for, but his most prized possession was his daughter, Philomena. She was his youngest child and the loveliest. Her eyes were darkest brown, her hair fell softly round her face like silk. Her skin was as soft as velvet. She sang like a nightingale and danced like a butterfly. But her most wonderful gift was her smile. When Philomena smiled everyone became happy. Her name means 'I am loved'.

One day Philomena came running to Midas. 'Father, there is a strange man at our gates. He is half man, half goat!'

Midas took Philomena by the hand, and walked to the gate. There stood Silenus, the satyr, the teacher of Dionysus, the god of wine.

Midas welcomed him: 'Silenus, I am honoured by your visit. Come in and rest from your journey.' Philomena smiled her welcome and the satyr's eyes lost their look of cunning and for once looked gentle as he smiled back at her.

Midas sent for servants to look after Silenus. He ordered the finest wines and food to be prepared for a banquet for his guest. Musicians and dancers entertained Silenus and the gentle splashing of fountains lulled him to sleep.

Silenus was grateful. The next day when he took leave of Midas and Philomena, he said to the king, 'King Midas, you have given me so much. I cannot leave without making you a present in return. What do you wish for? You may ask for anything.'

Midas thought and thought.

He was a greedy man and yet now when he had such an opportunity to fulfil his wildest dreams, he did not know what to ask for. What about the finest horse in the world? A horse who would ride more swiftly than Pegasus, the flying horse of the gods? What about a palace that would be famous as one of the wonders of the world? At last he spoke:

'Silenus, you are too generous, I cannot think of anything unless . . .'

'Well, come on, speak your wish,' commanded Silenus.

'No, I — er, I cannot,' Midas hesitated again, trying to sound as if he wanted nothing when he really wanted more than a man has the right to ask for.

'Are you sure?' asked Silenus, with his cunning eyes gleaming.

'I, er . . . need more time,' said Midas.

'Very well,' replied Silenus. 'I must leave you now, but remember my gift. Your wish will be granted whatever it may be.' Midas and Philomena walked with Silenus to the gate. Then Philomena ran back to the palace to find her nurse. Midas stayed in the garden, deep in thought.

Midas strolled under the trees, shaded from the brilliant sun. Suddenly he looked up at the sky. He gazed at the sun's rays and thought:

'The light of the sun is so wonderful. It seems that everything it touches turns to gold. How I wish I had such power!'

Midas returned to his throne room. He called to a servant to bring him water. The servant returned with a bronze cup. As Midas touched it, it turned to gold. He was dumbfounded until he remembered. 'My wish, my wish! Silenus has kept his promise. But have I really the power to turn everything I touch to gold?'

Midas ran round the room touching the pillars, the tables, the chairs. They all turned instantly to gold.

'It works, it works!' he cried. 'I shall be the wealthiest man the world has ever known!'

He danced, he shouted, he ran through his palace touching everything he could. Soon the palace was ablaze with golden light. 'How rich I am!' he shouted in triumph.

Exhausted, he returned to his throne room and sat down. He lifted the golden cup to his mouth. No water poured on to his parched lips, only a bitter, golden powder.

'Bring me wine!' he shouted. 'This water tastes like mud. Bring me peaches!' A servant returned with wine and a bowl of fruit. King Midas picked up a peach but as he bit into it he screamed, 'This peach is as hard as stone!' He looked at it, and it too had turned to gold. Another servant poured him wine but like the water, it was thick and bitter. Midas seized the servant in his rage.

The man stood stock still. He had turned to gold. But Midas did not see what had happened. Midas was crowing with pride. 'I am as rich as Zeus!' he shouted.

Dazzled by the light flashing from the golden throne and the pillars all around him, deaf to everything in the world except the sound of his own thoughts, he did not see Philomena coming towards him: 'Father, what is all this?' Midas bent down to lift her into his arms. 'Philomena, look, look around you. Is it not wonderful? Everything I touch turns to gold!'

But Philomena could say nothing. She too had turned to gold. Midas looked down at Philomena.

He touched her face, but her skin was like ice, her hair felt like thorns, her smile was an ugly grin. His tears fell so that they formed golden blisters on her cheeks.

'What have I done? Dionysus, forgive my greed! Philomena is more precious to me than all this gold could ever be.'

For many days and nights King Midas lay weeping on the ground, until his tears formed a golden pool beside him. Seeing his despair, Dionysus took pity on him. He ordered the king to bathe in the River Pactolus. Midas dragged himself to the river. The waters took away his terrible gift and for ever after the sands on the river bed glittered with gold.

Midas walked humbly back to his palace, stopping from time to time to touch a tree or a stone. His touch did not change them. As he neared the palace garden, he saw a girl dancing as lightly as a butterfly, he heard a laugh as sweet as the nightingale's song and saw a smile that warmed away his unhappiness. It was Philomena.

Miriam Hodgson   *A Touch of Gold*

Questions

1 Describe Philomena.
2 Who was Silenus?
3 What did he give Midas and why?
4 What did Midas do with this gift?
5 What happened when Midas tried to eat and drink?
6 What was the worst thing that happened?
7 How was it put right?
8 What did Midas learn from his experience?
9 This story was told by the ancient Greeks. Is there anything we can learn from it today?

Fight the fire!

40

How to play

Equipment

1. Dice, or spinner, or roller

How to make a spinner

a) Copy this diagram onto a piece of cardboard:

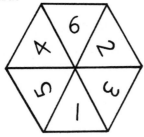

b) Cut it out.
c) Push a pencil stub or piece of twig through the centre.

How to make a roller

a) Get a six-sided pencil.
b) Write the numbers 1–6 on the sides.

2. Different coloured counters for the players

How to make a counter

a) Copy this drawing onto a piece of cardboard:

b) Colour it.
c) Cut it out.

Rules

1 The game can be played by two, three, or four people.
2 Each player throws the dice. The player with the highest score starts.
3 To move, you throw the dice and move your counter that number of squares.
4 Miss a turn if you land on a square with this sign:

5 You miss two turns if you land on a square with this sign:

6 If you land on a square marked , you move in the direction of the arrow, the number of squares shown.
7 The winner is the player who gets back to the fire station first.

Storytelling

You can use this game to help you make up a story about being a fireman.

Preparation

1 Play the game on your own.
2 As you play, write down the numbers of the squares you land on.
3 Continue playing until you reach square 56.
4 Go over the route you followed. This time, make a list of the things that happened to you.
5 Some numbers will have nothing against them (for example 4, 19, 33, 37 in the picture). For each of these, make up something that happened to you.

Writing

6 Now you are ready to start. You are the fireman. Tell the story of what happened to you from the moment when the alarm bell went until you got back to the fire station.

2 slid down pole
4
6 Got stuck in traffic jam. Had to wait
12 Got stuck at level crossing. Had to wait until train went through
13 Arrived at fire
19
23 Put on breathing apparatus
27 Driven back by flames
30 Rescued injured child
33
37
39 Carried child down ladder
50 Fire out - fire engine left
53 Had flat tyre
56 Arrived back at fire station

Only a game

What's the game?

In the pictures there are ten games being played. What is each one called? Write the names of the games.

What are the rules?

Choose four games from the pictures and number them. Copy and complete this table:

	Game 1	Game 2	Game 3	Game 4
Name of game				
Number of players				
Any special equipment				
Aim of the game				
What happens				

Sorting games

The games we play can be put into different **categories**. For example there are **indoor** games and **outdoor** games.

1   Copy this table and fill in the spaces with as many different games as you can think of. (You don't have to stick to the games in the pictures.) Some games have been put in to help you.

	Played by teams	Played by individuals
Indoor	skittles	snooker
Outdoor	football	tennis

2   Now do the same for this table:

	Physical game	Mental game
Indoor	table tennis	chess
Outdoor		

3   Now think of another set of categories. Make up a table using your new categories.

How do you play?

Improvising games

The MacDonald family are keen games players. When they went on holiday to the seaside last year they discovered that they had left all their games equipment at home. The first day of the holiday was a Sunday and all the shops were shut so they couldn't buy anything. They looked around on the beach, but all they could find was this:

Two pieces of wood each about 1′6″ long and 3″ wide

An old tennis ball

A lot of seashells

Some empty plastic containers

A few sticks of different lengths

A piece of fishing net

A piece of rope about 4 yards long

Games you know

Suppose you had been on holiday with the MacDonalds. How many games that you already know can be played with this equipment?

1 Make a list of the games.
2 For each one explain briefly what you would use and how you would use it to play the game.

Made-up games

Can you make up a game to be played using this equipment? Think up a game and describe how it is played. You should be able to answer these questions:

1 What is it called?
2 How many players?
3 What equipment does it use?
4 What space does it need?
5 What is the aim of the game?
6 How do you play?
7 What are the main rules?
8 How do you know when someone has won?

Making up a board game

You can make up a board game, like *Fight the fire!* on page 40.

1 The game will tell the story of someone trying to achieve something. Choose a subject. Here are some suggestions:
   Make a hit record!
   Win the F.A. Cup!
   First week at school!

> First Week at School

2 Make a list of the good things that happen. These will be the forward moves.

> Make a new friend
> Doing computer studies and cookery – great!
> New teacher likes you!
> Escaped from Bully Davies at Junior school
> Get into top set for Maths

3 Make a list of the bad things that happen. These will be the backward moves.

> Put in different class from best friend.
> Get lost and miss English lesson
> Sandwiches are stolen – hungry at dinner time
> Get into a fight

4 Decide what the finish of the game is.

> The weekend at last!

5 Draw out the board.

6 Write in the details of all the squares.

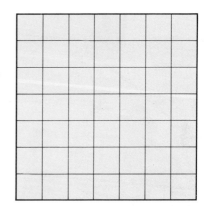

47

Sports day

Use your senses!

You have five senses: hearing, touch...

1 What are the other three?
2 Imagine you are standing where Salima is. What can you hear? Write down the sounds.
3 Now make a list for the other four senses.
4 Now make 'sense' lists for John, **or** Penny, **or** Daniel.

Who got the best view?

Salima, John, Penny, and Daniel are all standing in different places. So they all get a different view of what's going on.

1 Choose one event (e.g. the tug-o'-war).
2 Choose two reporters (e.g. Salima and Daniel).
3 Explain how they got different views of what happened.
4 Who got the best view?
5 Now do the same thing for a different event and two different reporters.

Overheard!

You are a reporter at the Sports. You are looking for 'human interest' stories. You listen in to people's conversations. The trouble is you only hear bits and pieces. So you have to make the rest up. For each of these conversations:

1 Decide who is speaking.
2 Decide what they are talking about.
3 Make up the whole conversation.

A – It's not my fault it broke!
  – You shouldn't have jumped on it.
  – I didn't mean to. I didn't know it was there.
  – You'll have to get her another one.

B – Is he always like that?
  – Only on Fridays.

Sports reports

Salima, John, Penny, and Daniel all wrote reports about the Sports.

Salima wrote a description of what it was *like*; what she heard, saw, smelled, tasted, and touched.

Penny remembered one of the conversations she had overheard. She imagined what the rest of it had been like and wrote a story about it.

John called his report, 'The Sports Day when everything went wrong'.

Daniel imagined that he was a famous newspaper reporter and wrote a famous newspaper report.

Choose one of the reporters and write his or her report.

49

What's your game?

Find the words

This word square contains the names of 12 games:

    7 outdoor games
    4 indoor games
    1 playground game

They may be across, up-and-down, or diagonally. They may be forwards or backwards.

F	H	S	R	U	G	B	Y
L	O	T	I	W	Z	L	V
L	C	O	G	N	I	B	D
A	K	D	T	N	N	C	F
B	E	U	S	B	H	E	O
T	Y	L	T	E	A	L	T
E	G	I	S	G	O	L	F
N	G	S	S	P	O	O	L

Which strip?

Fownhope Athletic shirts have narrow horizontal stripes. They wear black shorts.

Linlithgow Town wear shirts with narrow vertical stripes and white shorts.

Purbright United wear a shirt with broad vertical stripes and white shorts.

Baldock Rangers shirts have broad horizontal stripes and they wear black shorts.

Neasden Rovers have shirts with narrow horizontal stripes and white shorts.

The other strip belongs to **Dilwyn Town**. Which one is it?

Who plays what?

Kate, Mike, Tim, and Alison have joined a sports club. They have to decide what game to play. They can choose between cricket, rounders, tennis, and athletics. Cricket is only played at weekends and you can only play tennis on Wednesdays and Fridays. You can play rounders any day except Tuesday, Saturday, and Sunday. Athletics happens on Saturdays.

Kate can only play on a Monday or a Thursday. Mike doesn't like team games and prefers to play at the weekend. Alison likes team games but isn't free at weekends or on Tuesdays. Tim can manage any weekday, but prefers not to play team games.

Which game does each one choose?

What's wrong here?

In the passage that follows, ten words have been replaced by words that don't belong. Which are the ten words that should not be there, and what words do you think should be in their place?

I went over to the rubbish ground on Saturday to see if Dave and Wayne were over there. We often have a banana of football on a Saturday or go up to our den. (It's down an old oak tree that no one else can chop, except us.) When I got there, I couldn't see any of my friends at all. In fact the whole city was almost full. I'd taken a ball with me, so I just started to kick it around, when this tiny kid came up. He just pushed me out of the way and grabbed the grass. He was about twice as big as me, so there wasn't a lot I could see about it. He was swimming off, kicking the ball, when suddenly the most incredible thing happened . . .

What do you think it was?

My party

My parents said I could have a party
And that's just what I did.

Dad said, 'Who had you thought of inviting?'
I told him. He said, 'Well, you'd better start writing,'
And that's just what I did

To:
Phyllis Willis, Horace Morris,
Nancy, Clancy, Bert and Gert Sturt,
Dick and Mick and Nick Crick,
Ron, Don, John,
Dolly, Molly, Polly —
Neil Peel —
And my dear old friend, Dave Dirt.

I wrote, 'Come along, I'm having a party,'
And that's just what they did.

They all arrived with huge appetites
As Dad and I were fixing the lights.
I said, 'Help yourself to the drinks and bites!'
And that's just what they did,
All of them:

Phyllis Willis, Horace Morris,
Nancy, Clancy, Bert and Gert Sturt,
Dick and Mick and Nick Crick,
Ron, Don, John,
Dolly, Molly, Polly —
Neil Peel —
And my dear old friend, Dave Dirt.

Now, I had a good time and as far as I could tell,
The party seemed to go pretty well —
Yes, that's just what it did.

Then Dad said, 'Come on, just for fun,
Let's have a *turn* from everyone!'
And a turn's just what they did,

All of them:
Phyllis Willis, Horace Morris,
Nancy, Clancy, Bert and Gert Sturt,
Dick and Mick and Nick Crick,
Ron, Don, John,
Dolly, Molly, Polly —
Neil Peel —
And my dear old friend, Dave Dirt.

52

Neil Peel
All on his own
Danced an eightsome reel.

Dick and Mick
And Nicholas Crick
Did a most *ingenious*
Conjuring trick
And my dear old friend, Dave Dirt,
Was terribly sick
All over the flowers.
We cleaned it up.
It took *hours*.

But as Dad said, giving a party's not easy.
You really
Have to
Stick at it.
I agree. And if Dave gives a party
I'm certainly
Going to be
Sick at it.

Kit Wright

Phyllis and Clancy
And Horace and Nancy
Did a song and dance number
That was really fancy —

Dolly, Molly, Polly,
Ron, Don and John
Performed a play
That went on and on and on —
Gert and Bert Sturt,
Sister and brother,
Did an imitation of
Each other.
(Gert Sturt put on Bert Sturt's shirt
And Bert Sturt put on Gert Sturt's skirt.)

Who did what?

What did each of these people do at the party?
  Nicholas Crick   John
  Phyllis   Dave Dirt
  Gert Sturt
Write one sentence about each one. ,

Writing

Make up a story about a party when
everything goes wrong. Tell it in one of these
two different ways:

1 As it is told by the **mother** or **father** of the
   child giving the party.
2 As it is told by a rather wicked boy or girl
   who is a **guest** at the party.

53

Party time

Preparing

You're going to organise a party for the children from a local school. Before you go any further, decide and write down answers to these questions:

1 Which school?
2 What age group and how many children?
3 What occasion — Halloween, Diwali, Christmas, or what?
4 Exactly where will the party be?

Games

For a successful party you need to prepare a lot of games. You need different kinds of games:

   team games
   pencil and paper games
   musical games
   games with prizes
   acting games

1 Make a list of as many games as you can for each group.
2 Make your games into a **programme**. Decide:
   a) the best order for them
   b) how long each one will last.
3 Choose one game and explain the rules clearly.

Music

What kind of music do you need?
Make a list of the music for your party.

Puppet show

At your party there will be an entertainment for the children. You have booked a puppet show.

1   Decide what story they are going to tell. Some ideas:
    Punch and Judy
    Cinderella
    an Anansi Story
    Jack and the Beanstalk
2   Tell the story.
3   Make up the words for one of the scenes. Write it as a script.
4   Draw the scenery and the puppets for your scene.

Food

At the party there will be lots to eat and drink. Think of what people like to eat and drink at a party.

1   Make a list of the food.
2   Make a list of the different drinks.

Decorations and prizes

1   How would you decorate the place where the party is held? Could you make special decorations for it? Explain what you would make and how.
2   Some of the games need prizes. These should be worth winning but not too expensive. Make a list of suitable prizes.

55

It's not fair!

Questions

1 What has happened in the story?
2 What do you think Mother said in picture 3?
3 What do you think the girl was thinking in picture 4?
4 What do you think Mother said in picture 7?
5 What did she say in picture 8?
6 Has anything like this ever happened to you?
7 What do you think happened next?
8 What would you have done?
9 How would you make the story end: picture A, B, C or D?

Fair and unfair

1 Do you think the girl behaved fairly? What are your reasons?
2 What is your opinion of how the mother behaved, and why?
3 What do you think of each of these ideas:
   — My bedroom is my own place. I can do what I like there.
   — A child's bedroom is just a place to sleep in. It should be kept as clean and tidy as the rest of the house.
   — Everybody ought to have a place in the house where they can go and people will leave them alone.
4 What do you think the girl and her mother ought to do to avoid rows like this?

Storytelling

Tell the story. You can be:
a) the girl
b) the mother
c) someone else
You must follow pictures 1–8. After that you can make up what you like.

Colin

When you frown at me like that, Colin,
And wave your arm in the air,
I know just what you're going to say:
'Please, Sir, it isn't fair!'

It isn't fair
On the football field
If their team scores a goal.
It isn't fair
In a cricket match
Unless you bat *and* bowl.

When you scowl at me that way, Colin,
And mutter and slam your chair,
I always know what's coming next:
'Please, Sir, it isn't fair!'

It isn't fair
When I give you a job.
It isn't fair when I don't.
If I keep you in
It isn't fair.
If you're told to go out, you won't.

When heads bow low in assembly
And the whole school's saying a prayer,
I can guess what's on your mind, Colin:
'Our Father . . . it isn't fair!'

It wasn't fair
In the Infants.
It isn't fair now.
It won't be fair
At the Comprehensive
(for first years, anyhow).

When your life reaches its end, Colin,
Though I doubt if I'll be there,
I can picture the words on the gravestone now.
They'll say: IT IS NOT FAIR.

Allen Ahlberg

Questions

1 Who is speaking in the poem?
2 How old is Colin?
3 What kind of things happen at his school?
4 Do you think you would like Colin? Why?

Reading aloud

1 Work with a partner.
2 Divide the poem between you, so that one says some lines and the other the rest.
3 Practise reading the poem until you think you have got it just right.

Unfair

When we went over the park
Sunday mornings
To play football
we picked up sides.

Lizzie was our striker
because she had the best shot.

When the teachers
chose the school team
Marshy was our striker.

Lizzie wasn't allowed to play,
they said.

So she watched us lose, instead . . .

Michael Rosen

Writing a poem

Write a poem called 'It's not fair!'

Preparation

1   Write a list of times when you have been
    treated unfairly.
2   Write a second list of times when you have
    treated other people unfairly.
3   Write a third list of things in the world
    today which you think are unfair.
4   Decide which of all these things to write
    about.

Writing

5   Now write your poem. You could start
    and end each verse with the same lines:
    I think it is not fair

    . . . .
    . . . .
    . . . .
    . . . .
    Don't <u>you</u> think that's unfair?

For example:

I think it is not fair
That some people have baths
With real gold taps,
While others die of thirst and hunger;
Don't <u>you</u> think that's unfair?

I think it is not fair
That pets are left to die
Each year after Christmas
Because their owners are bored with them;
Don't <u>you</u> think that's unfair?

Look at it from my point of view . . .

Questions

These two pictures show two different versions of the same room.

1   Whose version is picture 1?
2   How would you describe it?
3   Whose version is picture 2?
4   How would you describe it?

Writing

Write two short descriptions based on the pictures. Each is called 'Our living room'. One is based on each version.

Writing from different points of view

Preparation

The boy and his parent had very different points of view about their living room. They actually **saw** it differently. Look at the picture on the opposite page. How would each of these people **see** the shopping centre?

    the policeman
    the thief
    the woman collecting for charity
    the teenagers
    the two old people on the bench

Writing

1   Choose two of the people in the picture. Write down their thoughts as they look around them.
2   Write a story about the picture. Write it as if you were one of the people in the picture.

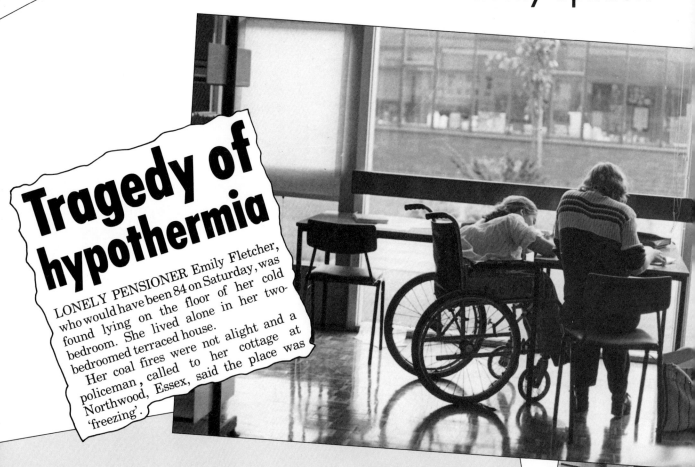

Tragedy of hypothermia

LONELY PENSIONER Emily Fletcher, who would have been 84 on Saturday, was found lying on the floor of her cold bedroom. She lived alone in her two-bedroomed terraced house.

Her coal fires were not alight and a policeman, called to her cottage at Northwood, Essex, said the place was 'freezing'.

In this city

In this city, perhaps a street.
In this street, perhaps a house.
In this house, perhaps a room.
And in this room a woman sitting,
Sitting in the darkness, sitting and crying
For someone who has just gone through the door
And who has just switched off the light
Forgetting she was there.

Alan Brownjohn.

What is your opinion?

1 Choose one of the items from here.
2 Write one or two sentences expressing your opinion about it.
3 Think about **why** you hold that opinion. Write down as many reasons as you can.
4 Now do the same for the other items.

Writing about the pictures

1 Choose one of the items to write about in more detail.

2 Prepare by writing in rough the answers to these questions:
  a) Exactly what is it illustrating?
  b) Why is it 'not fair'?
  c) What should be done about it?
  d) What could you do about it?

3 Now write a full account of your opinions and thoughts.

Writing about your opinions

1 Copy out one of these titles. Change it or finish it so that it describes what you want to say.
    What makes me really angry is...
    If I had my way...
    If I could, I'd ban...
2 Make a list of:
  a) your opinions about the topic
  b) your reasons
3 Now write a full account of your opinions and thoughts, with the reasons behind them.

63

Two stories

In these two stories a number of words have been missed out.
Read the stories and work out the best word to go in each of the
spaces. Write the number of each space and the word you have
chosen.

There is a different time scale

Nasrudin went to a Turkish bath. As ___1___ was poorly
dressed the attendants ___2___ him in a casual manner, gave
only a ___3___ of soap and an ___4___ towel.

   When he left, Nasrudin gave the two ___5___ a gold coin
each. He had not complained, and they could not ___6___ it.
Could it be, they wondered, that if he had been better ___7___
he would have given them an even larger ___8___?

   The following week the Mulla ___9___ again. This time, of
course, he was ___10___ after like a king. After being massaged,
perfumed and treated with the utmost ___11___, he left the bath,
handing each attendant the smallest possible ___12___ coin.

   'This', said Nasrudin, 'is for last time. The gold coins were for
this time.'

The burden of guilt

Mulla Nasrudin and his wife came home one day to find the
house burgled. Everything ___13___ had been taken away.

   'It is all your ___14___,' said his wife, 'for you should have
made ___15___ that the house was locked before we ___16___.'

   The neighbours took up the chant:

   'You did not ___17___ the windows,' said one.

   'Why did you not expect this?' said ___18___.

   'The locks were faulty and you did not ___19___ them,' said a
third.

   'Just a moment,' said Nasrudin, 'surely I am not the only one to
___20___?'

   'And *who* should we blame?' they shouted.

   'What about the thieves?' said the Mulla.

Idries Shah   *The Pleasantries of the Incredible Mulla Nasrudin*

Caught!

These days I wake up in the morning really looking forward to school and that's because I'm enjoying making my puppet. It's coming on really well, as I pile on layer upon layer of wet sticky newspaper, shaping and smoothing till paste oozes everywhere. It takes time, for you need a lot of layers. But, at last, I think I've done enough and I dry out the head on a tray on the radiator. Then Miss cuts the head for me with a Stanley knife, I don't like this bit much, I feel that I shall hear a scream coming from him, but the plasticine comes out like a ripe conker from its shell. The papier-mâché is several layers thick, and it sticks back together easily. And the good bit, painting the face, dead white to begin, then leave it to dry, then the black eyes and red dripping mouth and the fangs, and black wool for hair. While it's drying, Miss Plum helps me to sew his velvet cloak, which isn't easy, but looks fantastic, with white felt hands sewn to the ends of the seams, with red talons on them. As we sew I work out a scenario with Rosie and Darren. And it's good.

JJ is still absent.

*   *   *   *   *

Later that week . . .

Rosie is away. JJ is back.

The morning is long and draggy and boring. I get half my Maths wrong and have to do it again, and Miss Plum tears a page out of my English book 'cos it's so untidy, and I just can't be bothered to turn on my Tom smile. The radio programme we have on Thursday must have been written by morons with the most awful snobby accents you've ever heard, and I get told off for drawing swastikas over my pamphlet. The end of the morning arrives after several thousand years, and after Haricot Stew, Haricot Spew would be a better name for it, and Prune Pudd, we have to go back to the classrooms because it's still sending down stair rods outside, the chess club is cancelled, and so are most of the other clubs, because a lot of the teachers are absent with flu. So I go to the activity area to look at my puppet, the one bright spot in a black day.

It's lying smashed on the floor. JJ is just moving away from it.

And my inside hurts as though someone has pushed a knife into my guts. Miss Plum is standing there, suddenly.

'Don't mind so much, Gowie. GOWIE!'

But I've gone. Past her, after him, into the drama area, through the cloakroom hard behind him as he runs. And part of me can see me running and the faces turning to watch, and the terrified face of JJ turning round to see if I am coming. And, brother, I am. I am coming to settle you for ever. I knock Heather out of the way, she falls screaming to the ground, and JJ runs out of the classroom into the cloakroom, and into the boys' new bog, where I have him, trapped, he can't get away, and I thump hell into him, so that he cries and bends and tries to protect himself, and leaps on to the cistern in a frantic effort to escape.

The top part cracks, breaks and drops to the floor in pieces. The new cistern. And I am quite suddenly calm as he stands shivering in front of me, looking at the wrecked cistern.

'Corby,' says a voice behind me.

'It's all right, Mr. Merchant. I'm coming.'

Jonathan Johns and I stand before the Headmaster. He looks cold and old.

'I am writing to your parents,' he is saying. 'They will have to pay for the damage. This kind of vandalism cannot be allowed to go unpunished.'

JJ is crying. I stare at the rain pouring outside and the Doctor Who plant.

66

'I am going to cane you, now,' the head continues. 'You will receive three strokes on each hand and then I shall write down what I have done in the punishment book. It is a long time since I wrote anything in there, because this is part of my task as a Headmaster that I do not enjoy. But damaging property that has only just been installed at considerable expense cannot be permitted. You are boys in the top class of the school and others follow your example.'

His voice is steady and calm and seems to come from a long way away. I do not feel that I am really there. This is not happening. I try not to think what my mother will say when she is asked to pay for the damage. I try not to think of the pain of the cane.

I think of Rosie and I wish that it hadn't happened, that the cistern wasn't broken, that JJ hadn't come back, that my puppet, my puppet wasn't broken, that it was yesterday and I was laughing with Rosie, that the school had fallen down last night at eight o'clock when I wished it had.

But I am still standing in front of the headmaster in his study on a rainy day, and he is bending the cane, testing it before he hits my hands.

Gene Kemp   *Gowie Corbie Plays Chicken*

Questions

1　Who is telling the story?
2　At the beginning of the story, what is he making?
3　What is he making it out of?
4　How does he feel about what he has made?
5　Who do you think Rosie is?
6　Who is JJ? (Look through the story and you can find out what the letters stand for.)
7　Why does the storyteller have such a bad morning?
8　What does JJ do after dinner?
9　How does the storyteller react?
10　The headmaster calls what they have done vandalism. Is it?
11　What thoughts does the storyteller have while the headmaster is talking?

Your opinion

1　Do you think they should have been punished like this?
2　If you had been the headmaster what would you have done?
3　Do you think this story is true to life?
4　What do you think happens next?

Writing

Think of an occasion when you have been treated unfairly (in or out of school), or make one up. Write the story of what happened making sure that you describe your thoughts and feelings at each stage.

Codes

Number code

In a number code you write all the letters of the alphabet in line. Write numbers on a line below. Begin with whatever number you want, like this:

A	B	C	D	E	F	G	H	I
5	6	7	8	9	10	11	12	13
J	K	L	M	N	O	P	Q	R
14	15	16	17	18	19	20	21	22
S	T	U	V	W	X	Y	Z	
23	24	25	26	27	28	29	30	

This is a *Number 5 code*. In it

CODE becomes 7 19 8 9

HELP becomes 12 9 16 20

Letter code

A letter code works in exactly the same way, except that you use letters on the bottom line instead of numbers. Begin with whatever letter you like:

A	B	C	D	E	F	G	H	I
V	W	X	Y	Z	A	B	C	D
J	K	L	M	N	O	P	Q	R
E	F	G	H	I	J	K	L	M
S	T	U	V	W	X	Y	Z	
N	O	P	Q	R	S	T	U	

You use the code by turning the top row of letters into the bottom row. So

CODE becomes X J Y Z

HELP becomes C Z G K

This is a *Letter V code*. In it *A becomes V*.

Frame code

For this you draw a frame and put the letters in it.

ABC	DEF	GHI
JKL	MNO	PQR
STU	VWX	YZ

You show the letter by drawing the section of the frame it is in and putting a dot to show the position of the letter. So

CODE becomes

HELP becomes

As with the other codes, you don't have to start with A. For example this is a *Frame E code*.

EFG	HIJ	KLM
NOP	QRS	TUV
WXY	ZAB	CD

A code story

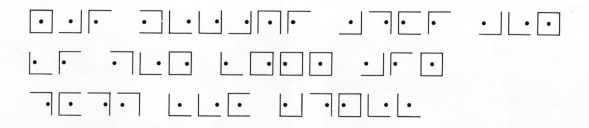

15 29 11 20 26 26 21 26 14 11 9 7 20 7 18 18 21 9 17 8 27 26 31 21 27
29 11 24 11 20 21 26 26 14 11 24 11. 15 26 14 15 20 17 15 7 19
8 11 15 20 13 12 21 18 18 21 29 11 10. 9 21 19 11 26 21 26 14 11
17 15 20 13'25 7 24 19 25 7 26 20 21 21 20 12 24 15 10 7 31.
16 7 25 21 20.

GYYN GY UN GCXHCABN UN NBY WUHUF VLCXAY. OLAYHN. GCFI.

I MUST ESCAPE. I NEED MONEY. I CANNOT MEET YOU — IT IS TOO
DANGEROUS. LEAVE MONEY IN THE USUAL PLACE. MILO.

This is part of a story. All we know is four coded messages and the codes that were used. Your job is to work out what happened and tell the story.

The codes

The codes used are:
  Letter U
  Number 7
  Frame G

What to do

Preparation

1 Decode the messages.
2 Work out the order in which they should be read.
3 Work out the story: what has happened to cause these messages?

Writing

4 Tell the story of what happened.

It's incredible!

You may have heard this story before, or spooky tales similar to it. This one has been told all round the country, but no one knows who told it first or whether it is true. What do you think: true or false?

Storytelling 1

Either: tell the version of the story you know.
Or: tell the story told in the pictures.

Preparation

1 Decide which story to tell.
2 Decide who is telling the story.
3 Decide where and when it happened.
4 Decide the main points of the story.

Writing

Now write your story.

Storytelling 2

Make up a ghost story to tell the rest of the class. Make up your own subject, or choose one of these:

    The ghostly postman
    The stranger at the railway station
    The story of the missing traffic warden

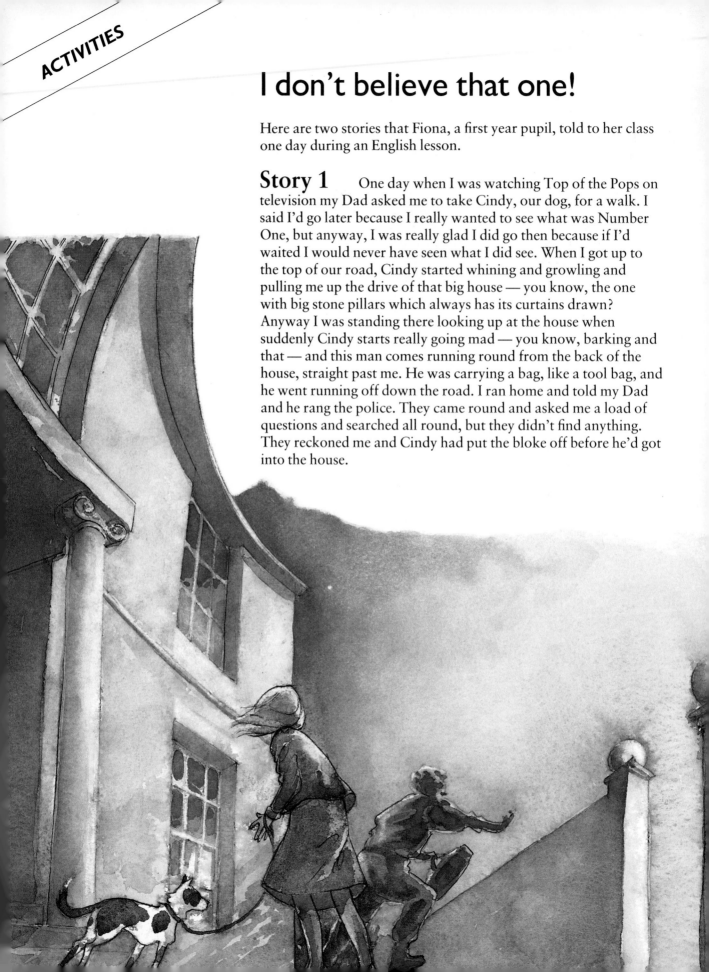

I don't believe that one!

Here are two stories that Fiona, a first year pupil, told to her class one day during an English lesson.

Story 1

One day when I was watching Top of the Pops on television my Dad asked me to take Cindy, our dog, for a walk. I said I'd go later because I really wanted to see what was Number One, but anyway, I was really glad I did go then because if I'd waited I would never have seen what I did see. When I got up to the top of our road, Cindy started whining and growling and pulling me up the drive of that big house — you know, the one with big stone pillars which always has its curtains drawn? Anyway I was standing there looking up at the house when suddenly Cindy starts really going mad — you know, barking and that — and this man comes running round from the back of the house, straight past me. He was carrying a bag, like a tool bag, and he went running off down the road. I ran home and told my Dad and he rang the police. They came round and asked me a load of questions and searched all round, but they didn't find anything. They reckoned me and Cindy had put the bloke off before he'd got into the house.

Story 2

Another time we were on holiday in Devon and we were staying in this old farm house. There was a big bathroom with a really old-fashioned bath and white tiles. It was always freezing cold in the bathroom. We had Cindy with us and every time she went in the bathroom she used to hang her tail between her back legs and sort of whimper and whine. Anyway, my sister reckoned the bathroom was haunted and she asked a woman who looked after the place and she said a girl had hanged herself in there about a hundred years ago and that sometimes when people looked in the mirror over the washbasin they saw her face behind them. So my sister wouldn't go in the bathroom by herself. Well, on the last night of our holiday, we were in the bathroom together, having a really quick wash, you know, when suddenly the lights started to flicker. We just ran out as fast as we could. So my Dad went to have a look and when he came back he said, 'Did you see anything in there?' We said, 'No, only the lights flickering.' And he said there was something funny going on and not to go back in there. So we were all really scared that night and in the morning we went home.

What do you think?

One of Fiona's stories is true and one isn't. Which is which?

1 Read the two stories again carefully.
2 For each one, make a note of anything that you find hard to believe.
3 Try to think of common sense explanations for all these things.
4 Decide which of the stories you think is true and why.
5 Write down your opinion and the reasons for it.

Storytelling

Make up two stories about yourself, following these instructions:

1 One story must be true and the other made up.
2 The true story should be as strange as possible.
3 The untrue story should be as believable as possible.

Tell your stories to the class.

What kind of stories do you like writing?

Ken

I like the kind of stories we tell each other at home. My dad knows hundreds of stories and he tells them to us. I like telling them to other people.

Shoshana

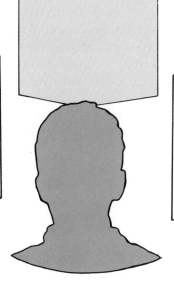

I like true stories best. I don't like it if I have to make one up. It's silly. I like writing about my own adventures, but sometimes I make them more exciting than they really were.

I'm best at stories which I make up. I like inventing characters who aren't a bit like me. I make them do incredible things. Sometimes the things they do are impossible really, but I don't care. I just let my imagination take over.

Marcia

I think my best stories are a bit true and a bit false. I mean they are about things which could happen but they haven't really happened to me. I usually write about girls who are like me but I put them in unusual places or funny situations.

Hayley

Questions

1 Suppose the face in the middle was you. What would you put in the speech box?
2 Which of the others do you agree with most and why?
3 Here are the titles of three stories. Which of the children do you think told each one?
   a) The day I became a TV star
   b) The worst day of my life
   c) The rescue in space
4 Which one would you choose?

Davina's dream

Making up a story

Davina dreams many kinds of story, as you can see. You are going to tell one of them.

Preparation

1 Look at the picture and let your imagination work on it.
2 Choose a part of the picture that you find interesting and make up a story about it.
3 Before you begin, think about the answers to these questions:

Who is the Teller? Is it an 'I' story?
Is the 'I' you, or a made-up person?
Is it a 'he/she' story?

When? Where? How much do you need to tell people about when and where it happens?
Who? Who are the main characters? How much do you need to tell people about them?

Writing

4 Now write your story.

True or false?

1   About 1900 some people said it was wrong to put books by men writers next to books by women writers — unless the writers were married.

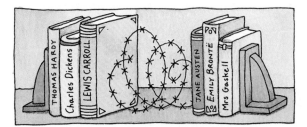

2   A queen of Sweden hated fleas. She planned to get rid of all the fleas in her rooms. She had a four-inch cannon made, with tiny cannon-balls, which she fired at every flea she saw.

3   One man was struck by lightning, not once or twice, but at seven different times.

4   In 1973 the oldest man in America was asked to be on television. He had to refuse because he could not leave his father who was ill.

5   The pencil on the right is longer than the pencil on the left.

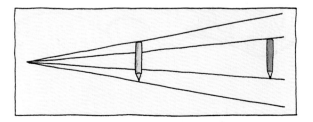

6   A kangaroo can jump higher than a house.

7 There are eight squares here.

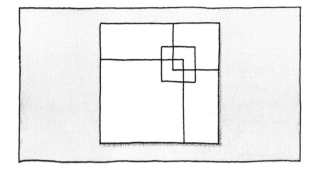

8 A man in Brazil was looking for a lost mule. He knew there was great danger from wild animals and he was very worried. At last he came across a huge snake, sleeping in the sun, and he saw what might be the outline of a mule inside the snake's body. He knew that the snake had killed the mule and then swallowed it whole.

9 Many, many years ago, a German baron was chasing some robbers on horseback. He followed them through the city gate and over the drawbridge. As the baron went after them through the gate, the portcullis dropped down, just missing the rider but chopping the horse in two. The baron was very quick-thinking. A laurel bush grew by the city gates, and the baron took some shoots from the bush and stitched his horse back together again. The horse was soon better, and the following spring the laurel shoots began to grow. From then on, the baron could travel in the hottest weather because the leaves of the laurel growing from the horse kept him in the shade.

What do you think?

For each of the 'facts' on these two pages:

1 Say whether you think it is true or false.
2 Explain as fully as you can why you think so.

A fall of snow

Jake Benson was a winter boy. Born one white January, with the snow falling heavily outside, just as it was now, he had turned his red, crumpled face to the window, and smiled to see it. Or so his mother claimed. Certainly he had always loved snow. Even now, as he sat looking miserably out of the classroom window, the sight of the tiny whirling flakes comforted him.

After all, he thought, it was Timothy's own fault. If he hadn't dawdled over his lunch, making patterns in his mashed potatoes with his fork, chasing each separate pea around his plate, we wouldn't have run into the bully-gang in the corridor. All the first form knew they were looking for a new victim. And there was Timothy, such an obvious choice, small and pale, his pink nose like a white rabbit's, twitching with terror.

What did he expect me to do? Jake thought. There were four of them, great third form louts, what could I have done? It'd just have made things worse. . . .

He glanced towards Timothy. Timothy was sitting hunched over his book, his chin in his hands, his fingers spread to hide the tear stains on his cheeks. He had not said a word since he had come back. He had avoided Jake's eyes ever since that last imploring look in the corridor after lunch, when the bully-gang had closed in on him.

'Hey, you! What's-yer-name, you with the fancy curls. We want a word with you!' they'd said, surrounding Timothy, herding him towards the door to the playground. And Jake had run away.

He did not see what else he could have done. They were both new boys, solitary boys, usually to be found on the edge of chattering groups, smiling uneasily. And because they sat next to each other in class, they had started going about together, waiting for one another so that they could travel on the same bus home.

But we're not friends exactly, Jake thought, I don't owe him anything.

Outside the window, the snow fell constantly, silently covering up the flawed concrete paths, the bedraggled winter hedges, covering up the stains of the day.

I'll make it up with him on the bus going home, Jake decided, I'll explain . . . what? That I'm a coward? That I was glad they'd picked on him and not on me? That I never even thought of telling one of the teachers. . . .

Oh hell, I'll make up something, some excuse. I'll say I tried to find Mr Tinker, old Stinker on playground duty, blind as a bat with the snow on his spectacles and no windscreen wipers. I'll think of something.

He did not have a chance. When the final bell went, Timothy snatched up his books and bolted. Jake, hurrying after him, was caught by Mr Becker with some silly query about his homework. When he got to the cloakroom, Timothy was not there.

'Timothy Sinclair? He's been gone ages,' one of the boys told him. 'Been crying, hadn't he?'

'Dunno,' Jake mumbled, and hurried away.

On the bus going home, he sat looking sadly out of the window. The snow, tarnished by the sodium lighting, was all trampled on the pavements. It fell lightly now, separate flakes that could do no more than speckle the ugly scraped areas outside the shops, where the earlier snow had been shovelled away into dirty heaps in the gutters.

Why do they always spoil it? Jake thought.

He got off at Tatten's Corner, and started to walk home. And there on the Common, the snow lay in all its glory; deep and crisp and even, like a Christmas carol. Bushes gleamed like white coral in the liquid dusk. The frozen trees stood out against the soft radiance of the snowlight, the earth brighter than the sky. Not a mark, not a footprint marred its innocent perfection.

Jake stood and stared at it longingly. Never cross the Common by yourself, his mother had warned him, and Jake had promised, remembering the headlines in the local paper: woman found stabbed, old man mugged, child missing.

Tonight, he hesitated. All that untrodden snow, just waiting for him! Why shouldn't he, just this once? He had had such a horrible day. And it was safe. No murderer or mugger could be hiding behind a bush, waiting to spring out on him. There was no way they could have got there without marking the snow. Not unless they could fly!

He glanced round. There was no one to see him.

Slowly Jake left the trampled pavement and the safety of the street lamps, and walked out on to the Common.

He was an Arctic explorer. He was a spaceman, setting foot on the frozen dust of some strange planet. He was a yeti, striding across the white wastes of the Himalayas. He was the king of Winter . . .

Who's that!

He was a small boy again, a frightened boy, swerving away from the figure that barred his way, trying to run and skidding . . . With a cry, he fell into a cold bed of snow and lay trembling. He looked up. It was only a snowman! A huge snowman standing like a sentinel beside the path. Those were just black pebbles in its head, that seemed to stare at him so threateningly. It was only compacted snow, not a white stocking over its face. Its ugly slit of a mouth was merely a small twig.

Jake got slowly to his feet and walked up to it. What an ugly mug! There was something familiar about those clumsy, lumpish features, the mean eyes, the thick shoulders . . . *Art Waller!* That's who it reminded him of! Art Waller, the leader of the bully-gang. Art Waller who had made him desert his friend. All the misery and shame of his day exploded into anger. He smashed his fist into the smirking white face, and saw with fierce joy the cold flesh crack. Half the head slid down over the huge shoulders and fell to the ground. Still the one remaining eye was fixed on him, with an unblinking stare. Plucking a half-buried stick out of the ground, he fell upon the figure, stabbing and slicing and smashing, kicking it with his feet. 'That's for Timothy!' he shouted. 'And that's for me! And that's for all of us you turn into cowards and sneaks! Take that!' When at last he stopped, flushed and panting, there was only a pile of battered snow at his feet. He turned away, feeling slightly sick, somehow ashamed. His boots crunched into the deep snow as he walked, but the pleasure had gone out of it. And he seemed to have strayed off the path; there were bushes in front of him, barring his way. He turned, meaning to retrace his steps. Turned and stood staring. There were footprints in the snow behind him. Not his own. Huge footprints, monstrous footprints! And they were moving. They were coming after him.

He could see no one. Nothing but the footprints, biting heavily into the deep snow to the cold earth beneath. There were the prints of animals as well. He saw the rosettes made by their invisible paws, running from side to side, as if sniffing him out.

In terror, he turned and ran, slipping and skidding, crashing into the frozen bushes, dislodging little avalanches of snow. And every time he looked over his shoulder, he could see the footprints hurrying after him, faster and faster. Now he came to a round clearing, a white circle like a huge spotlight. As he hesitated, wondering which way to go, he saw footprints coming out of the bushes in front of him; from every side they came, closing in on him. With a cry of despair, he raced to the nearest tree. His gloved fingers scrabbling on the frozen bark, somehow he managed to pull himself up on to a branch. When he looked down, he saw the footprints had encircled the tree. Here and there, there was a soft flurry in the snow, as if some large, invisible animal had sat down to wait. The wind howled like wolves in the branches. And all the time, a terrible sense of evil steamed up from the ground below him. It was as if by his own violence, by smashing the snowman, he had let loose an answering violence in the night. He could not hold on for long. Already he could no longer feel the branch beneath his fingers and his legs were becoming numb. Sooner or later he would slip and fall, and he knew when he did, it would be the end of him. He tried to call for help, but all that escaped his cold lips was his panting breath, sending up little smoke signals of distress into the freezing air. It seemed the most terrible thing of all that it was the snow that had betrayed him, the snow he had always loved. The world tilted before his eyes. He felt his fingers slipping. Help me, he prayed. And suddenly it began to snow again, tiny flakes, each no bigger than the head of a pin. Faster and faster they fell, in thousands and millions, tumbling from the dark sky. And the footprints began to move once more, running backwards and forwards as if trying to escape. The tiny flakes were smothering them, obliterating them; already they were no more than shallow indentations, scampering about in panic. Still the snow fell remorselessly, wiping them out. There was nothing below Jake, as he tumbled out of the tree, but a smooth, immaculate whiteness. He lay there, stiff as an icicle, his hot tears freckling the snow beneath his cheek. The snow fell gently on him, covering him, hiding him. He had only to shut his eyes and lie, safe in this soft, cold bed, and nothing could ever hurt him again. But even as he thought this, a lump of snow, falling from the tree, slapped his face. He could hear the whisper of the flakes as they hit his anorak, trying to tell him something. Little fingers of ice poked him.

'What d'you want me to do?' he said aloud, and sat up, brushing the snow from his clothes, beating his cold legs with his colder hands, until they came back to life.

All around him, the snow flakes whispered, in the trees, in the bushes, but he could not understand what they were saying.

When at last Jake staggered off the Common and down the pavement, he saw a boy standing under the lamp-post outside his house. It was Timothy, his hands in his pockets, the hood of his anorak pulled tightly around his small, pale, unsmiling face. Jake walked up and stood in front of him, not speaking.

'Why're you hobbling like that?' Timothy asked.

'Fell out of a tree.'

'Daft.'

'Yeah. Wanna come in with me?'

'Might as well.'

They turned and walked together towards the lighted house.

'Sorry about — you know, after lunch,' Jake said awkwardly.

Timothy shrugged: 'Nothing you could do.'

Was there really nothing? Jake wondered.

The snow fell on them as they walked, freckling their anoraks, forming white epaulettes on their shoulders. Jake held out his hand and saw the flakes fall, and melt, and fall again until his navy woollen glove was covered. Funny stuff snow, he thought, weak and wet and soft — and yet so powerful!

Suddenly he smiled. He knew at last what the snow was trying to tell him. There *was* something. In his mind he saw an avalanche of first form boys, falling upon the bully-gang. The whole of 1a and 1b and 1c, joining together to smother them, to wipe them out for ever.

John Gordon

Your writing

And that's just what happens: tell the story of
'The day the bullies met their match'.

Where is Titch Turner?

Titch Turner lives at 73B Mossford Road. On Thursday 23rd June she left school at the usual time — 3.40. It usually takes her about ten minutes to walk home. At quarter past five her mum got home as usual, but Titch wasn't there. Her dad got home just after six, but she still wasn't home. Mr and Mrs Turner decided that they had better go to the police and tell them their daughter was missing. They spoke to WPC Andrews.

WPC Andrews

Imagine you are WPC Andrews. You need to find out about Titch.

1   Make a list of what you would need to know.
2   How would you get this information? Write a list of questions that you would ask Mr and Mrs Turner.

Mr and Mrs Turner

What answers would Titch's parents give to the questions? Use the information on this page to help you work out the answers. You may need to make up some of the answers, but make sure that they fit in with the information you have.

The interview

WPC Andrews questions Mr and Mrs Turner. You can either *act* this conversation with a partner, or *write* it as a script.

Where could Titch be?

The police have to think what Titch might have done after leaving school.

What's wrong?

In each of these picture stories Titch has done something wrong. For each one explain what it is and why it is wrong.

Telling the story

Imagine you are Titch. For each of these stories:

1 Decide what she was thinking about as she decided not to go straight home.
2 Decide exactly what she did.
3 Decide what happened in the end.
4 Tell the story as if you were her.

When did you last see her?

The police questioned all Titch's friends and anyone else who might have seen her. They found six people who had seen her.

'... about half past five. She came along Harbury Road and crossed over the roundabout into Harbury Lane. Then she went into the flats there.'

'I was walking along the canal towpath and I saw a little girl playing under the bridge – where Eastway goes over the canal. I didn't think much of it – children often play under that bridge ...'

'I saw her going out of the school playground at quarter to four. She was going towards the foot-bridge – you know the one that goes over the dual carriageway. She was on her own.'

'... It must have been about quarter to five. She was walking along the side of the dual carriageway. Derby Way, it's called. Just before it goes over the canal. It's very dangerous there because there isn't a proper footpath and the traffic goes so fast along there ...'

'That's the girl I saw mucking about on that building site on Harbury Road. I'm sure it was her. What time? Oh about five o'clock I suppose ...'

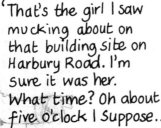

'Yes I saw her. She was playing on the swings in the recreation ground. She was there for five or ten minutes ... at about four o'clock.'

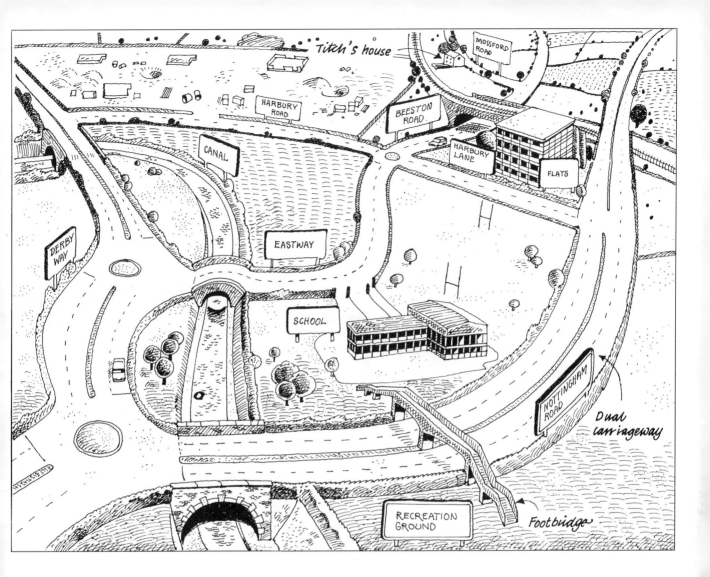

Where did she go?

Use the statements and the map to work out:

1 Where Titch went.
2 When she was in each place.

Copy this timetable and fill it in.

Time	Place

What happened?

Now you know where Titch went and when she was in each place, decide what you think happened to her. Tell the story in two ways:

1 How the police (or her parents) eventually found her.
2 **Her** version of what she had done and why — write it as if she was telling her parents all about it.

Dreaming

SPACE CADET, JOHNNY JET SETS OFF IN SEARCH OF THE OTHERS...

Gosh!

Your tea's on the table, John.

...SUDDENLY, A VENUSIAN VENTOSAURUS APPEARS!

Wow!

I think that boy must be deaf sometimes!

JOHNNY TURNS AND RUNS FOR COVER...

BUT MISSING HIS FOOTING JOHNNY STUMBLES!

INSTINCTIVELY HE CLUTCHES HIS RAY-GUN! JOHNNY SHOOTS...!

ZAP!

Didn't you hear me? Your tea's ready! You've always got your head in a comic!

Always living in a dream world!

Hello Son!

But Hank, what do you mean?

I want you to marry me Mary-Sue, and I can take you away from all this!

...We can live on my ranch in Texas!

Questions about the story

1 What does John's mother think of him reading his comic?
2 What does he think when she takes it away?
3 What kind of TV programme are his parents watching as he eats his tea?
4 What is their attitude as they watch?
5 How does this compare with what John has been doing with his comic?
6 If you had to make up a title for this story, what would you call it?

Thinking about day-dreaming

1 In the story, John is day-dreaming. Why do people day-dream?
2 Is it a good thing, or a bad thing, to do?
3 Are there any differences between John's day-dreaming and his parents'?

Finding out what people think

Ask friends and family about day-dreaming. Ask them whether they day-dream and if so, when, and what they day-dream about.

Make notes of what they tell you, so that you can report back to the rest of your group or class.

Telling a story

You're going to tell a story about someone who is always dreaming. She has such a vivid imagination that these day-dreams completely take over her life.

Preparation

1 Think of the main character and give her a name.
2 Think of some of the things that your character dreams about.
3 Think of things that might start off these day-dreams.
4 Think of what might happen to your character if she was so wrapped up in these dreams that she completely forgot where she was and what she was supposed to be doing.

Writing
Now join all these ideas up into a story.

The monster poem

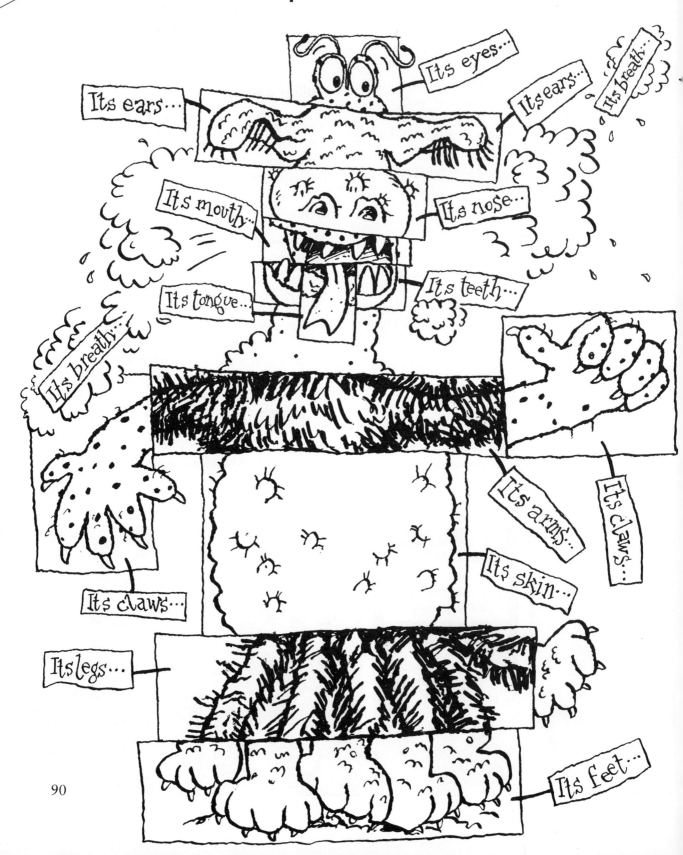

When people want to describe something they often compare it to something else. This kind of comparison is called a **simile**.

He's got a face like the back of a bus.

Her feet are as flat as pancakes.

Questions

1 Think of some more well-known similes and write them down.
2 Write a sentence explaining what a simile is.
3 Look at the drawing of the monster. Choose two of the labels. Copy each one down and finish it by using a simile.

Writing a monster poem

In your poem you have to find similes which no one has ever used before. Here's the poem that Rachel and Alison wrote.

The drawing lists some of the things to write about. But you can think of others. What about the monster's smell, the way it moves, what it sounds like . . . ?

1 Choose some of these things to write about.
2 For each one invent a new simile to describe it.
3 Use these when you write your poem.

MONSTER POEM.

His hair is like a bed of straw,
  All matted and in a tangle.
His ears are as big as a dragon's claws,
  That stick out at a right angle.
His eyes are as brown as a donkey's coat,
His mouth is like a castle moat,
His nose is as long as a snooker cue.
  And bulbous too.
His skin is as green as a grassy meadow.
  It spreads a ginormous shadow.

His tongue is like a mouldy cake,
His teeth are as sharp as a garden rake.
His body is like a slimy slug,
His neck is wrinkled like the nose of a pug.
His legs are like the stumps of trees,
With knot holes in for his knobbly knees.
His arms are round and fat, like the body of a huge cat.
His feet, which pong of rotting cheese,
Are as wrinkled and scarred as his knobbly knees.

by Rachel Young and
Alison Carey

NiGHT is THE TiME

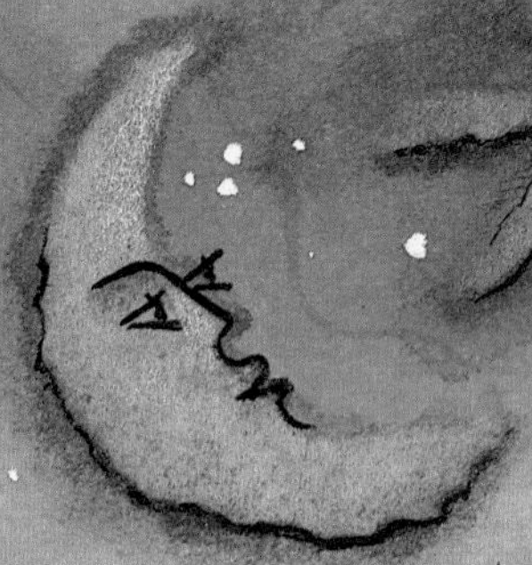

I like to stay up

I like to stay up
and listen
when big people talking
jumbie* stories

Ooooooooooooooooooh
I does feel so tingly
and excited
inside — eeeeeeeeeee

But when my mother say
'Girl, time for bed'
then is when
I does feel a dread

then is when
I does jump into me bed
then is when I does cover up
from me feet to me head

then is when
I does wish
I didn't listen
to no stupid jumbie* story
then is when
I does wish
I did read me book instead

Grace Nichols

* *jumbie* — ghost

Only the moon

When I was a child I thought
The new moon was a cradle
The full moon was granny's round face.

The new moon was a banana
The full moon was a big cake.

When I was a child
I never saw the moon
I only saw what I wanted to see.

And now I see the moon
It's the moon
Only the moon, and nothing but the moon.

Wong May

FOR DREAMING

Four moons

The cowboy's moon is thin and clear,
A lazy C on a midnight steer.

Robin Hood's moon lets planets go
Like burning arrows from his bow.

Over the sea the pirate's moon
Glitters like a gold doubloon.

But the spaceman's moon is round and white
Like a porthole on the side of night.

Dennis Doyle

Thinking about the poems

1   Which poem did you like best and why?
2   These poems want you to make pictures in
    your imagination. Choose **part** of one
    poem that made it easy to see pictures in
    your mind.
    a)   Write it down.
    b)   Describe what you can imagine when
         you read it.

Describing things in different ways

Four moons and *Only the moon* describe the
moon in many different ways.

1   How is the moon described in *Only the
    moon*?
2   How is it described in *Four moons*?

Now try to do the same thing yourself:

3   Write down at least four different ways of
    describing *fog*.
4   Write a poem with the title *Only the fog*.
5   How would each of these people think
    about *snow*?
    a) a granny
    b) a child
    c) a postman
    d) a blind man
6   Use these ideas to write about *A snowy
    day*.

Words

Heroic words

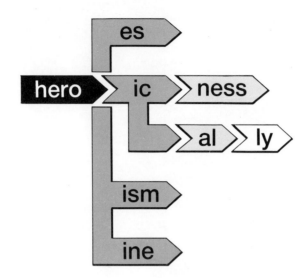

This is a word-building chart.

1 Use it to make as many words as you can with **hero** in them.
2 What is special about the spelling of the plural of hero? (One hero, two hero__ ?)

Fright words

1 This is a list of words with **fright** in them:
frighten, frightening, frightful, frightened, frightfully, frights, frighteningly, frightener, frightfulness
2 Make up a word-building chart for fright.

Help words

1 Make a list of all the words you can think of that contain **help**.
2 Use a dictionary to check your list and add to it.
3 Make up your own word-building chart for help.

Super words

1 Look at these words: **super**man
     supermarket
What do you think **super** means in them? Use that idea to work out what these words mean:
     superhighway
     superpower
     superstar
2 Look at these words: **super**sonic
     supernatural
What does **super** mean in them? Use this meaning of **super** to work out what these words mean:
     superhuman
     superimpose (*impose* means 'put on')
     superstructure (*structure* means 'something built')

Dream words

1. Write each of the words on a separate line.
2. Against each one write down what you think it means.
3. Use a dictionary to correct or add to your definitions.
4. Choose words from the list to fill the blanks in these sentences:
   a) When I fell asleep last night I had a terrifying _____ : I dreamed I was being chased by the _____ of a dead headmaster.
   b) The travellers in the desert thought they had found water, but it was only a _____ .
   c) I had a lovely _____ in Maths yesterday — I imagined I was playing tennis at Wimbledon.
   d) The drugs I was given for my illness had a strange effect on my _____ . I kept having _____ s of brightly coloured monsters.

Scared words

This is a list of words about being scared:

    afraid   horrified frozen   scared
    panicky   alarmed   startled shocked
    frightened petrified

1. If there are any you don't know, look them up in the dictionary.
2. They all have different *strengths:* **petrified** is much stronger than **scared**. Make up a league table with the strongest at the top and the weakest at the bottom.
3. Make a diagram of **scared** words, like the one for **dream** words. Choose words from the list or think of new ones. Make the words look like their meanings.

The Dream

Once upon a time there was a merchant who lived in Baghdad. He had a most beautiful house. It stood at the end of a cobbled street and was surrounded by a fine large garden full of palm trees. The house was built round a courtyard paved with grey marble, and in the centre of the courtyard stood a white marble fountain. The merchant had once been rich, but he had fallen upon hard times and had gradually lost all his money. He was forced to do the hardest labouring jobs in order to stay alive.

One night, after a hard day's work, he fell asleep exhausted. It seemed that his head had hardly touched the pillow when he had the most peculiar dream. He saw a young man, dressed in blue, who spoke to him. 'Don't be unhappy,' he said. 'Your troubles are over. Travel to Cairo and there you will make your fortune.'

When the merchant woke up he remembered the dream, but he thought to himself, 'Who'd believe a dream like that? Make my fortune in Cairo indeed! What nonsense!' And off he went to work as usual. That night he had the same dream. Still he didn't take any notice, telling himself that he didn't believe in dreams.

On the third night the young man in blue appeared to him again and told him the same thing: 'Go to Cairo and there you will make your fortune.' The dream was so vivid and the man in blue seemed so sincere that at last the merchant was persuaded. 'After all,' he told himself, 'what have I got to lose? My life here in Baghdad is wretched. My beautiful house is falling into disrepair. Even if the dream proves to be untrue I shan't be any worse off than I am now.'

So, early the next morning, he set off for Cairo. The journey took many weeks and was difficult and dangerous, but eventually he reached the city. It was late in the evening when he arrived and he couldn't find anywhere to sleep. In the end he came to a mosque and decided to spend the night in the courtyard.

While he was asleep, a gang of robbers came into the mosque. They made a hole in the wall and broke into the house next door. The owners of the house were woken up by the noise and shouted for help. This alarmed the robbers, who ran away. After some time the police chief and his men arrived. They went into the mosque and found the merchant lying there, still asleep. They grabbed hold of him and beat him up, then carried him off to prison.

The merchant lay in the prison for three days until the police chief had him brought out for questioning. Hungry and dirty, the poor merchant was dragged before him.

'Where do you come from?' demanded the police chief.

'Baghdad.'

'So what are you doing in Cairo?'

'I have come to seek my fortune.'

'What makes you think that your fortune lies in Cairo?'

'I had a dream and in it a young man dressed in blue told me: "Go to Cairo and there you will make your fortune." So I came.'

'And have you made your fortune?'

'No. My only fortune so far is that I was beaten up by your men.'

The police chief burst out laughing at the merchant's stupidity. 'You fool!' he roared. 'It serves you right for believing in dreams. Listen: I had a dream about a young man in blue. He told me to go to Baghdad and look for a house at the end of a cobbled street. He said it had a beautiful garden full of palm trees. The house was built round a grey marble courtyard in which there was a white marble fountain. He told me to dig beneath the fountain and I would find a huge sum of money buried. What nonsense! Do you think I believed it? I had the same dream three times, but I'm not such a fool as to think it's worth travelling all the way to Baghdad to look for a house with a white marble fountain. Go on — get out of here and go back to your home. Get yourself a proper job and stop thinking about dreams and fortunes.'

With that, the police chief ordered his men to release the merchant and send him on his way. The merchant promptly started off for Baghdad. He had listened very carefully to what the police chief said. As soon as he got back to his house, with its grey marble courtyard, he began to dig under the white marble fountain. There — just as the police chief had been told in the dream — he found a huge sum of money in gold and silver.

The merchant was able to set up in business again and lived happily for the rest of his life. And the police chief? He knew nothing of all this and continued to believe that dreams were nonsense.

Thinking about the story

1 There are five pictures in the story. Give each one a title. (If possible, choose your words from the story.)

2 There isn't a picture for the last part of the story. Describe what you think should be in it.

Writing

The police chief and the merchant had two different ideas about dreams. What's more, the police chief never did find out what happened to the merchant. After the merchant goes home, the police chief tells one of his friends about this crazy man from Baghdad. Write the story he tells.

Jack and the Beanstalk

Stories are like trees. The main trunk is the story you know. The branches are the different stories you could make up, starting from the story you know.

In this special, the trunk is the story of Jack and the Beanstalk. The branches are some of the stories that **could** happen to Jack and his mother. They branch out from the story you know.

What you do

1 Find number 1.
2 Read the beginning of the story.
3 Follow the trunk. When it branches, follow the branch.

4 Read what the branch says, then make up the rest of that story. You could:
   tell it to a friend
   or remember it for later.
5 Then go back to the trunk and follow it, as before, branching off whenever you can.
6 By the time you get to the end you will have made up many different versions of Jack and the Beanstalk: which one did you like best?

Writing

Choose the one you liked best and tell it as a complete story.

The man offers him three wishes...

The man is an outlaw...

The man says "Come with me..."

2A

2B

2C

2

On the way, Jack meets a man.

2D

Jack and his mother are very poor. All they have is one cow. Jack's mother tells him to take the cow to market and sell it for as much as he can get.

1

1A On the way the cow dies. Jack goes home...

The man buys the cow and gives Jack a magic spinning wheel...

Jack climbs up a little way and

a) falls to the ground and is knocked unconscious. He dreams a strange dream...

b) picks some giant beans. His mother cooks them... **5B**

Jack hates heights, so his mother starts to climb the beanstalk instead... **5A**

In the morning Jack wakes up and sees that a huge beanstalk has grown up in the night. It goes up into the clouds.

Jack sleeps and sleeps and sleeps...

5

4A
Jack's mother is furious. She throws the beans out of the window into the garden and sends Jack to bed.

4C The beans are eaten by the chicken...

4

4B The beans fall into the well, where a frog finds them...

The man offers Jack some magic beans in exchange for the cow. Jack takes the beans and sets off for home.

3

3A Jack never reaches home. He is later found in a ditch. The beans have gone...

Then she locks him in a dungeon, where there are already three other children. They plan their escape...

The Giant's wife is very unhappy. She likes Jack and she wants him to stay...

The Giant discovers Jack and tells him the sad story of his life...

Jack picks up a poker and creeps up behind the Giant...

Jack begins to feel very strange indeed.
(a) Soon he falls to the ground, unconscious...

(b) Then he notices that he has begun to grow...

(7A)

(7B)

There is a loud noise. The Giant is coming: Fee, Fi, Fo, Fum... he can smell the blood of a stranger. Jack hides quickly.

(6A)

(6B)

(6C)

(7)

Jack climbs up the beanstalk and eventually comes to the Giant's Castle. The Giant's wife lets him in and gives him some food.

(7C) The Giant has a very sensitive nose. He begins to sniff Jack out. He gets closer and closer...

(6)

100

The rest of the story is lost in the clouds. You will have to make it up for yourself. See if you can make up some branches as well.

At last the Giant goes to sleep. Jack creeps up to him and steals the gold. He runs back to the top of the beanstalk.

9C There is a rumbling and a barking. The Giant has woken up and is chasing after Jack, with his giant dog...

9B Just as he is about to climb down he hears the sound of chopping- his mother is chopping the beanstalk down...

9A The gold is too heavy for Jack to carry far, and he hears the Giant coming. He quickly digs a hole at the top of the beanstalk and buries the gold...

9

The Giant's wife calms the Giant down. After his supper, he begins to count his gold.

8B As he counts it, he lists all the people he has stolen it from, and describes how he got it from them...

8A

(@) he is very cruel and he is going to do all sorts of nasty things...

As he counts it, he says aloud all the things he is going to do with it:

(b) he is very kind and is going to use his gold to help people...

Brian Walker

Variations

1 Work with a partner and make up the stories together.
2 Work in a small group and see how many different stories you can make up, using the tree, and working as a team.
3 As a group, prepare to tell the rest of the class some of your best stories.
4 Choose another well-known story and make a story tree out of that.

Then what happened?

A It all began when I was late getting up one day. By 8.15 mum had already called me three times. I could hear her clattering around in our spotlessly clean kitchen. I knew that soon she would be thumping up the stairs to pull the bedclothes off...

Questions

The pictures tell you how Sue's story started. Then there are three different ways in which it might have continued.

1 What is the story in Version B?
2 How do you think it might continue?
3 What is the story in Version C?
4 How do you think it might continue?
5 What is the story in Version D?
6 How do you think it might continue?
7 Which do you think looks most interesting and why?

Writing

Preparation

1 Choose the version of the story that you want to finish.
2 Write a list of the main things that happen after the pictures end.
3 Copy out the words beginning the story ('It all began when I was late . . .' etc).

Writing

4 Now tell the rest of the story.

Deciding on the story

When you are writing a story you have to decide on a lot of things: for example, who is telling it, and where and when it happens. One of the most important things to decide is the main outline of the story. Very often you will find that your first ideas aren't always the best. This is a way of thinking of more than one storyline.

Suppose your story started like this:

A It all began when I was late getting up one day. By 8.15 Mum had already called me three times. I could hear her clattering around in our spotlessly clean kitchen. I knew that soon she would be thumping up the stairs to pull the bedclothes off…

The story could continue like this…

..or it could go on like this..

…or like this …

B She shouted up, 'Are you coming down, or have I got to come upstairs and drag you out of bed?' That's always the last warning she gives me, so I decided I'd better get a move on. I started to dress, but I couldn't find half my clothes, so it was ages before I found my way down to the kitchen. Mum was furious. She was so angry she wouldn't let me have any breakfast.

C At last I got out of bed, dressed and wandered downstairs, still half asleep. I didn't feel at all hungry, but Mum always makes me eat something for breakfast, so I went into the kitchen. As I opened the door, I got the shock of my life. Sitting in the kitchen was a man I'd never seen before in my life.

D At last I dragged myself out of bed. I didn't bother to wash, but just threw my clothes on and hurried out of my bedroom onto the landing. I'm not sure what happened next. I think I must have tripped on the mat or something. Anyway, the next thing I knew, I was lying at the bottom of the stairs with my leg twisted under and screaming with pain.

E He seemed very much at home. As I came in he smiled and said, 'Hallo Sue.' He had an American accent.
'Hallo,' I said. 'Who are you?'
'This is Jim,' said Mum. 'He's an old friend of your Dad's. From the time when Dad was working in Canada.'

F I looked at him and then I looked at Mum. She looked as if she'd been crying. The man seemed rather embarrassed.
'What's the matter, Mum?'
'It's bad news, Sue. Very bad news'.
'Why? What's happened?'
'It's your Dad. He's-' Mum broke off and started to cry.

Making a plot chart

This diagram shows several different ways the story of Sue and her mum could go. You can use a plot chart like this to help you improve a basic story you have thought of.

1   Choose a story you have thought of. (It could be your own story about Sue.)
2   Copy the outline of the plot chart. (You may need more than one page.)

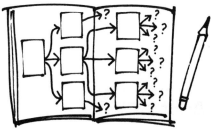

3   Write the first stages of your story in the middle boxes of your plot chart.

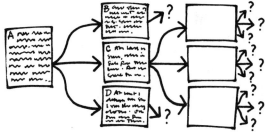

4   Now make up variations to fill in the empty boxes.

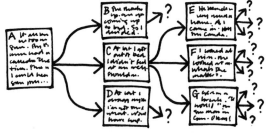

5   If you get stuck, or when you have finished, show your plot chart to a partner and ask for her/his comments.
6   When you have finished, choose the variation you like best and make up a story based on that.

Problem page

Dear Aunt Agatha,

I hope you will be able to help me with a problem. It's about my friend Pat. Pat's dad has been out of work for a long time, and the family are all very hard up. A week ago she and I were sorting out some clothes for the School Jumble Sale. We went through all the clothes to make sure that no one had left anything in the pockets. We didn't find much, until we got to the very last thing, a man's suit. I found a £10 note in the top pocket. I showed it to Pat and then put it on the table to give to our teacher Mr Morris when he came back from having his coffee. When Mr Morris came back I told him about the money, but when I went to get it, it wasn't there any more. We looked everywhere, but it had simply disappeared. Pat said that we had thrown a lot of rubbish away after putting the money on the table and we must have thrown it away by mistake. I don't believe that, though, because I threw the rubbish away and I checked it very carefully to make sure that we weren't throwing away anything worth having. Pat was looking a bit embarrassed about all this, but Mr Morris said not to worry about it. I can't help worrying, though. Pat and I were the only people in the room and from the look on her face, I'm sure she must have taken it. I don't blame her, really - her family is so hard up - but stealing <u>is</u> stealing.

What is the best thing to do?

Yours,

Dermot

Dear Aunt Agatha,

I have a problem and I hope you will be able to help me with it. I have a very close friend called Anna and some time ago she lent me her favourite record. It's a double album by the Squeegees. When she lent it to me she made me promise that I would look after it very carefully and <u>never</u> lend it to anyone else.

Everything was fine until the other day. I kept the record in with my other records and wouldn't even let my parents play it (not that they wanted to!) Then my other friend Katherine came to see me. We were playing records, but not Anna's of course. My mum came in and asked me to pop down to the shops to get some bread. When I got back I found that Katherine was playing Anna's record. Worse than that - there was a big scratch on one side. I'm sure it wasn't there before. Katherine said she didn't do it and that it wasn't her fault.

What shall I do? Anna is my best friend. If I had enough money I would buy her another one, but the album costs £10, and I can't afford that much. Please help me!

Yours,

Hilary

106

Dear Aunt Agatha,

I am writing to you to ask you for your advice about a very difficult problem.

There's recently been a lot of trouble at our school about stealing. Someone has been going to the classrooms during break and taking sweets, pens and money from people's bags and cases. The Headmistress has said that no one is allowed to stay in the classrooms at break time, but things are still being stolen. So now the headmistress has said that if anything else is taken, the whole class will be punished.

Last Wednesday I left my drink and bag of crisps in the classroom at break. I was so thirsty I decided to risk being caught and go back into the room to get them. I got in there without being seen and to my surprise I saw Peter XXXXXX my best friend. He was bending over and taking something out of Sandra Powell's bag. When he saw me he was very embarrassed. Then he said that Sandra had asked him to get it for her. I didn't believe that – they've been enemies ever since they've been at the school.

The trouble is, Peter and I have been friends ever since I can remember. I don't want to report him. But he was definitely stealing from Sandra's bag. I don't see why the whole class should suffer. What shall I do?

Michael Parry

What would you do?

Read the three letters carefully. For each one:

1. Make a list of the different things that could be done by the person who wrote the letter.
2. For each of these, work out the good and bad points.
3. Decide which of these **you** would do, and why.

Writing

Choose one of the three problem letters and write Aunt Agatha's reply.

The happy man's shirt

This story is divided into sections. The first section is printed at the beginning, but the others are in the wrong order. Read them all and work out the right order.

1   There was once a wealthy king who had a son whom he loved very much. Unfortunately this prince was very unhappy. He spent all his time mooning around the palace or staring out of the window and feeling sorry for himself. The king tried everything he could to make his miserable son happy — parties, outings, new clothes, but nothing would make him smile.

2   First a priest was brought to him.
    'Are you truly happy?' asked the king.
    'Certainly, Your Majesty.'
    'What would you say if I made you my bishop?'
    'Your Majesty I should be delighted!'

3   He asked the young man to stay just where he was and hurried off to fetch his courtiers. He brought them back to where the young man was. He spoke to him again.
    'I'll give you anything you want,' he said, 'if only you will help me.'
    'If I can, I will.'
    'It's my son. He is so unhappy and only you can help him.'

4   'Then you must ask him to change shirts with your son.'
    'That will make my son happy?'
    'Certainly, Your Majesty.'
    So the king sent messengers all over the kingdom and all over the world, seeking for a truly happy man.

5   'Then you're no use to me. Go away — I'm looking for someone who is so happy that he doesn't want to change in any way.'
    So the hunt went on. Every time the messengers brought someone to the king, he tested them in the same way. But without success, until someone told him that the king of a nearby country was a truly happy man.

6   Eventually they came back to the king with their solution.
    'Your Majesty,' said their leader, 'we have thought very carefully about your son, and this is what we have decided. You

108

must search the kingdom for a happy man; a man who is so happy that there is nothing on earth that would make him happier.'

'And then?' asked the king.

7   So the messengers returned to their own land without asking that king for his shirt.

The king was very sad. To cheer himself up he went hunting. While he was out in the forest, he stopped for a rest and came upon a young man who was working on his farm and singing as he worked. Unseen, the king watched him as he worked. He had never seen anyone who looked so happy. He approached the young man.

'Good morning,' he began.

'Good morning, Your Majesty.'

8   'How?'

'Your shirt — I want your shirt.' And the king rushed up to the young man and began to tear off his jacket. Then, as he undid the last button and the jacket fell open, he stopped and stared in disbelief.

The happy young man was wearing no shirt at all.

9   The king sent out an order calling all the wise men and doctors of the kingdom to come to his palace. He brought the prince to them and explained what the problem was. The wise men examined the prince and talked to him for a while. Then they went away and discussed the whole problem.

10   'You seem a very happy young man. How would you like to come to my palace and work for me. I would pay you very well and give you a splendid house to live in.'

'That's very kind of you, Your Majesty,' said the young man, 'but I couldn't think of it. I wouldn't even want to change places with you yourself. You see I am perfectly happy the way I am.'

'At last!' thought the king, 'I have found a perfectly happy man.'

11   The king sent his messengers to meet him. When he talked to them he said, 'Yes. I really am the happiest man in the world. There's just one thing that bothers me. I'm so happy that I'm afraid of the day when I shall have to die and leave all this happiness behind me. That makes me sad.'

retold from *Italian Folktales* by **Italo Calvino**

William's Version

William and Granny were left to entertain each other for an hour while William's mother went to the clinic. 'Sing to me,' said William.

'Granny's too old to sing,' said Granny.

'I'll sing to you, then,' said William. William only knew one song. He had forgotten the words and the tune, but he sang it several times, anyway.

'Shall we do something else now?' said Granny.

'Tell me a story,' said William. 'Tell me about the wolf.'

'Red Riding Hood?'

'No, not *that* wolf, the other wolf.'

'Peter and the wolf?' said Granny.

'Mummy's going to have a baby,' said William.

'I know,' said Granny. William looked suspicious.

'How do you know?'

'Well . . . she told me. And it shows, doesn't it?'

'The lady down the road had a baby. It looks like a pig,' said William. He counted on his fingers. 'Three babies looks like three pigs.'

'Ah,' said Granny. 'Once upon a time there were three little pigs. Their names were —'

'They didn't have names,' said William.

'Yes they did. The first pig was called —'

'Pigs don't have names.'

'Some do. These pigs had names.'

'No they didn't.' William slid off Granny's lap and went to open the corner cupboard by the fireplace. Old magazines cascaded out as old magazines do when they have been flung into a cupboard and the door slammed shut. He rooted among them until he found a little book covered with brown paper, climbed into the cupboard, opened the book, closed it and climbed out again. 'They didn't have names,' he said.

'I didn't know you could read,' said Granny, properly impressed.

'C — A — T, wheelbarrow,' said William.

'Is that the book Mummy reads to you out of?'

'It's my book,' said William.

'But it's the one Mummy reads?'

'If she says please,' said William.

'Well, that's Mummy's story, then. My pigs have names.'

'They're the wrong pigs.' William was not open to negotiation. 'I don't want them in this story.'

'Can't we have different pigs this time?'

'No. They won't know what to do.'

'Once upon a time,' said Granny, 'there were three little pigs who lived with their mother.'

'Their mother was dead,' said William.

'Oh, I'm sure she wasn't,' said Granny.

'She was dead. You make bacon out of dead pigs. She got eaten for breakfast and they threw the rind out for the birds.'

'So the three little pigs had to find homes for themselves.'

'No.' William consulted his book. 'They had to build little houses.'

'I'm just coming to that.'

'You said they had to *find* homes. They didn't *find* them.'

'The first little pig walked along for a bit until he met a man with a load of hay.'

'It was a lady.'

'A lady with a load of hay?'

'N O! It was a lady-pig. You said *he*.'

'I thought all the pigs were little boy-pigs,' said Granny.

'It says lady-pig here,' said William. 'It says the lady-pig went for a walk and met a man with a load of hay.'

'So the lady-pig,' said Granny, 'said to the man, "May I have some of that hay to build a house?" and the man said, "Yes." Is that right?'

'Yes,' said William. 'You know that baby?'

'What baby?'

'The one Mummy's going to have. Will that baby have shoes on when it comes out?'

'I don't think so,' said Granny.

'It will have cold feet,' said William.

'Oh no,' said Granny. 'Mummy will wrap it up in a soft shawl, all snug.'

'I don't *mind* if it has cold feet,' William explained. 'Go on about the lady-pig.'

'So the little lady-pig took the hay and built a little house. Soon the wolf came along and the wolf said —'

'You didn't tell where the wolf lived.'

'I don't know where the wolf lived.'

'15 Tennyson Avenue, next to the bomb-site,' said William.

'I bet it doesn't say that in the book,' said Granny, with spirit.

'Yes it does.'

'Let me see, then.'

William folded himself up with his back to Granny, and pushed the book up under his pullover.

'*I* don't think it says that in the book,' said Granny.

'It's in ever so small words,' said William.

'So the wolf said, "Little pig, little pig, let me come in," and the little pig answered, "No". So the wolf said, "Then I'll huff and I'll puff and I'll blow your house down," and he huffed and he puffed and he blew the house down, and the little pig ran away.'

'He ate the little pig,' said William.

'No, no,' said Granny. 'The little pig ran away.'

'He ate the little pig. He ate her in a sandwich.'

'All right, he ate the little pig in a sandwich. So the second little pig —'

'You didn't tell about the tricycle.'

'What about the tricycle?'

'The wolf got on his tricycle and went to the bread shop to buy some bread. To make the sandwich,' William explained, patiently.

'Oh well, the wolf got on his tricycle and went to the bread shop to buy some bread. And he went to the grocer's to buy some butter.' This innovation did not go down well.

'He already had some butter in the cupboard,' said William.

'So then the second little pig went for a walk and met a man with a load of wood, and the little pig said to the man, "May I have some of that wood to build a house?" and the man said, "Yes."'

'He didn't say please.'

'"Please may I have some of that wood to build a house?"'

'It was sticks.'

'Sticks *are* wood.'

William took out his book and turned the pages. 'That's right,' he said.

'Why don't you tell the story?' said Granny.

'I can't remember it,' said William.

'You could read it out of your book.'

'I've lost it,' said William, clutching his pullover.

'Look, do you know who this is?' He pulled a green angora scarf from under the sofa.

'No, who is it?' said Granny, glad of the diversion.

'This is Doctor Snake.' He made the scarf wriggle across the carpet.

'Why is he a doctor?'

'Because he is all furry,' said William. He wrapped the doctor round his neck and sat sucking the loose end. 'Go on about the wolf.'

'So the little pig built a house of sticks and along came the wolf — on his tricycle?'

'He came by bus. He didn't have any money for a ticket so he ate up the conductor.'

'That wasn't very nice of him,' said Granny.

'No,' said William. 'It wasn't *very* nice.'

'And the wolf said, "Little pig, little pig, let me come in," and the little pig said, "No," and the wolf said, "Then I'll huff and I'll puff and I'll blow your house down." And then what did he do?' Granny asked, cautiously.

William was silent.

'Did he eat the second little pig?'

'Yes.'

'How did he eat this little pig?' said Granny, prepared for more pig sandwiches or possibly pig on toast.

'With his mouth,' said William.

'Now the third little pig went for a walk and met a man with a load of bricks. And the little pig said, "*Please* may I have some of those bricks to build a house?" and the man said, "Yes." So the little pig took the bricks and built a house.'

'He built it on the bomb-site.'

'Next door to the wolf?' said Granny. 'That was very silly of him.'

'There wasn't anywhere else,' said William. 'All the roads were full up.'

'The wolf didn't have to come by bus or tricycle this time, then, did he?' said Granny, grown cunning.

'Yes.' William took out the book and peered in, secretively. 'He was playing in the cemetery. He had to get another bus.'

'And did he eat the conductor this time?'

'No. A nice man gave him some money, so he bought a ticket.'

'I'm glad to hear it,' said Granny.

'He ate the nice man,' said William.

'So the wolf got off the bus and went up to the little pig's house, and he said, "Little pig, little pig, let me come in," and the little pig said, "No," and then the wolf said, "I'll huff and I'll puff and I'll blow your house down," and he huffed and he puffed and he huffed and he puffed but he couldn't blow the house down because it was made of bricks.'

'He couldn't blow it down,' said William, 'because it was stuck to the ground.'

'Well, anyway, the wolf got very cross then, and he climbed on the roof and shouted down the chimney, "I'm coming to get you!" but the little pig just laughed and put a big saucepan on the fire.'

'He put it on the gas stove.'

'He put it on the *fire*' said Granny, speaking very rapidly, 'and the wolf fell down the chimney and into the pan of water and was boiled and the little pig ate him for supper.'

William threw himself full length on the carpet and screamed.

'He didn't! He didn't! *He didn't!* He didn't eat the wolf.'

Granny picked him up, all stiff and kicking, and sat him on her lap.

'Did I get it wrong again, love? Don't cry. Tell me what really happened.'

William wept, and wiped his nose on Doctor Snake.

'The little pig put the saucepan on the gas stove and the wolf got down the chimney and put the little pig in the saucepan and boiled him. He had him for tea, with chips,' said William.

'Oh,' said Granny. 'I've got it all wrong, haven't I? Can I see the book, then I shall know, next time.'

William took the book from under his pullover. Granny opened it and read, *First Aid for Beginners: a Practical Handbook.*

'I see,' said Granny. 'I don't think I can read this. I left my glasses at home. You tell Gran how it ends.'

William turned to the last page which showed a prostrate man with his leg in a splint; *compound fracture of the femur.*

'Then the wolf washed up and got on his tricycle and went to see his Granny, and his Granny opened the door and said, "Hello, William."'

'I thought it was the wolf.'

'It was. It was the wolf. His name was William Wolf,' said William.

'What a nice story,' said Granny. 'You tell it much better than I do.'

'I can see up your nose,' said William. 'It's all whiskery.'

Jan Mark   *Nothing to be afraid of*

Writing your own stories

1 Write your own version of the story of the three little pigs in which the pigs are the 'baddies' and the wolf is a 'goody'.
2 Write your own version of a popular story, changing it in the way that William does.
3 Granny tells William another story and he interrupts in the same way. Tell the story of what happens. You can choose the story that Granny tells, or pick one from this list:
   Red Riding Hood
   Cinderella
   The Babes in the Wood
   Puss in Boots

114

Reference Section

Planning and drafting 1

When you are writing a story, it is very difficult to do your best work straight away. You usually need to plan before you write and then change what you have written.

Getting your ideas together

You are going to write a story about the boy in the picture.

1   Look at the other pictures carefully. You must use at least one of them in your story.
2   Choose the picture(s) you are going to use.
3   Write down the ideas that come to you as you look at your picture(s).

```
fed up
wants to go to America
goes to the docks
```

4   Think about a story that connects the boy and the picture.
5   Write down the most important things about the story.

```
He has run away from home
He wants to go to America.
He goes to the docks.
He hides behind some crates.
He tries to get on the ship.
He gets caught
```

Writing a first draft

Now it's time to start writing your story. Don't worry about getting it all exactly right. Just write the story as fast as you can. To make it easier later on, only write on every third line:

```
Jason was fed up, both his parents were
always shouting at him, his mother naged him.
School was awful. He was fed up! He dicided to
run away to america then they would miss him
all right.
```

Building it up

When you have finished your first draft, read it through and think about it. Even better, get a friend to read it and tell you what s/he thinks about it. Don't worry about the spelling and punctuation, just think about making the story better. Write the new ideas on the spare lines:

```
                    had had enugh
Jason was fed up, both his parents were
                    his mother had been on at him all day
nagging him to do jobs around the house, yesterday
                    his father
always shouting at him, his mother naged him
had shouted at him for nothing at all
                                            that
School was awful. He was fed up! He dicided to
                    had had enugh
he would run away.
run away to america then they would miss him
    he wood go to america, Then they wood be sory
for all the unkind things they'd said to him
all right
then they would miss him alright.
```

Planning and drafting 2

Thinking about words

By now your writing probably looks a bit of a mess. It's time to start sorting it out. Begin by looking at all the words. Ask yourself two questions:

1 Have I chosen the best words?
2 Are they spelled right?

Choosing the best words and checking spelling are covered on pages 120–123. Copy out your story, changing the words as you go:

Jason had had enough, his mother had been on at him all day, pestering him to do jobs around the house, yesterday his father had sworn at him for nothing at all. School was so boring he might as well be dead. He had had enough!

He decided that he would run away. He would stow away on a boat to America, Then they would be sorry for all the unkind things they'd said to him. Oh yes: Then they would miss him all right.

Punctuating

All that's left is to make sure that you have got the punctuation right. The rules of punctuation are on pages 124–125. Read through your writing and correct the punctuation as you go:

Jason had had enough. His mother had been on at him all day, pestering him to do jobs around the house,. Yesterday his father had sworn at him for nothing at all. School was so boring he might as well be dead. He had had enough!

He decided that he would run away. He would stow away on a boat to America,. Then they would be sorry for all the unkind things they'd said to him. Oh yes: then they would miss him all right.

Presentation

Now your story is finished. It doesn't *look* very finished, though, because it contains a number of corrections. So if you want other people to be able to read it and enjoy it, you need to make a fair copy. This one could be illustrated, as well.

Jason's escape

Jason had had enough. His mother had been on at him all day, pestering him to do jobs around the house. Yesterday his father had swom at him for nothing at all. School was so boring he might as well be dead. He had had enough!

He decided that he would run away. He would stow away on a boat to America. Then they would be sorry for all the unkind things they'd said to him. Oh yes: then they would miss him all right.

Summary

These are the main stages in planning and drafting:

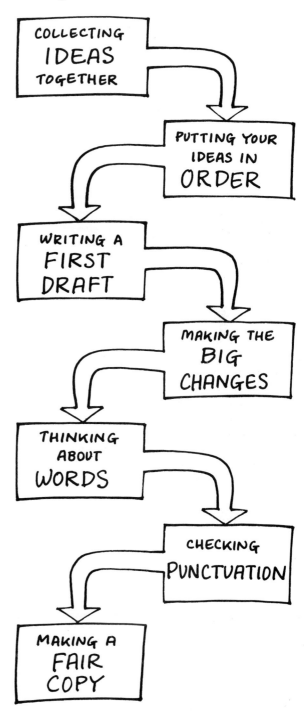

COLLECTING **IDEAS** TOGETHER

PUTTING YOUR IDEAS IN **ORDER**

WRITING A **FIRST DRAFT**

MAKING THE **BIG CHANGES**

THINKING ABOUT **WORDS**

CHECKING **PUNCTUATION**

MAKING A **FAIR COPY**

Words: using a dictionary

gewgaw (g- *as in* get) *n.* a showy but valueless ornament or fancy article.

geyser *n.* **1.** (*pr.* gy-zer) a natural spring sending up a column of hot water or steam at intervals. **2.** (*pr.* gee-zer) a kind of water-heater.

ghastly *adj.* **1.** causing horror or fear, *a ghastly accident.* **2.** (*informal*) very unpleasant, very bad, *a ghastly mistake.* **3.** pale and ill-looking. **ghastliness** *n.*

ghat (*pr.* gawt) *n.* (in India) **1.** a flight of steps down to a river, a landing-place. **2.** a mountain pass; *Eastern and Western Ghats,* mountains along the east and west coasts of south India.

ghee (g- *as in* get) *n.* Indian clarified butter, made from the milk of buffaloes or cows.

gherkin (ger-kin) *n.* a small cucumber used for pickling.

ghetto (get-oh) *n.* (*pl.* ghettos) a slum area occupied by a particular group, especially as a result of social or economic conditions.

ghost *n.* **1.** a person's spirit appearing after his death. **2.** something very slight; *he hasn't the ghost of a chance,* he has no chance at all. **3.** a duplicated image in a defective telescope or a television picture. —*v.* to write as a ghost-writer. —**ghostly** *adj.,* **ghostliness** *n.* □ **ghost town,** a town abandoned by all or most of its former inhabitants. **ghost-writer** *n.* a person who writes a book, article, or speech for another to pass off as his own. **give up the ghost,** to die.

ghoul (*pr.* gool) *n.* **1.** (in Muslim stories) a spirit that robs graves and devours the corpses in them. **2.** a person who enjoys gruesome things. **ghoulish** *adj.,* **ghoulishly** *adv.*

giblets (jib-lits) *pl. n.* the edible parts of the inside of a bird, taken out before it is cooked.

giddy *adj.* (giddier, giddiest) **1.** having the feeling that everything is spinning round. **2.** causing this feeling, *giddy heights.* **3.** frivolous, flighty. **giddily** *adv.,* **giddiness** *n.*

gift *n.* **1.** a thing given or received without payment. **2.** a natural ability. **3.** an easy task. □ **gift token,** a voucher (given as a gift) for money to buy something. **look a gift-horse in the mouth,** to accept something ungratefully, examining it for faults.

gifted *adj.* having great natural ability.

gift-wrap *v.* (gift-wrapped, gift-wrapping) to wrap attractively as a gift.

gig [1] (g- *as in* get) *n.* a light two-wheeled horse-drawn carriage.

gig [2] (g- *as in* get) *n.* (*informal*) an engagement to play jazz etc., especially for a single performance.

giga- (jy-gă) *prefix* one thousand million.

gigantic *adj.* very large. **gigantically** *adv.*

giggle *v.* to laugh in a silly or nervous way. —*n.* **1.** this kind of laugh. **2.** (*informal*) something amusing.

gigolo (jig-ŏ-loh) *n.* (*pl.* gigolos) a man who is paid by an older woman to be her escort or lover.

gild [1] *v.* (gilded or gilt, gilding) to cover with a thin layer of gold or gold paint. **gild the lily,** to spoil something already beautiful by trying to improve it.

gild [2] *n. see* guild.

gill (*pr.* jil) *n.* one quarter of a pint.

gillie (gil-i) *n.* a man or boy attending someone shooting or fishing in Scotland.

gills (g- *as in* get) *n.* **1.** the organ with which a fish breathes in water. **2.** the vertical plates on the under-side of a mushroom cap. □ **green about the gills,** looking sickly.

Alphabetical order

Words in a dictionary are arranged in alphabetical order:

1 of first letter: **g**host is before **h**airy
2 then of second letter: g**h**ost is before g**i**ddy
3 and so on: gho**s**t is before gho**u**l

At the top of each page are printed the first and last words on that page.

Pronunciation

A dictionary gives advice about how to speak the word.

> **ghoul** (*pr.* gool) *n.* **1.** (in Muslim stories) a spirit that robs graves and devours the corpses in them. **2.** a person who enjoys gruesome things. **ghoulish** *adj.,* **ghoulishly** *adv.*

Meaning

The dictionary tells you the meaning of a word.

> **ghee** (g- *as in* get) *n.* Indian clarified butter, made from the milk of buffaloes or cows.

If there is more than one meaning, it gives each one a number.

> **geyser** *n.* **1.** (*pr.* gy-zer) a natural spring sending up a column of hot water or steam at intervals. **2.** (*pr.* gee-zer) a kind of water-heater.

Spelling

Sometimes a dictionary also gives help with spelling.

> **giddy** *adj.* (giddier, giddiest) **1.** having the feeling that everything is spinning round. **2.** causing this feeling, *giddy heights.* **3.** frivolous, flighty. **giddily** *adv.,* **giddiness** *n.*

Exercises

Alphabetical order

1 Write out each of these groups of words in alphabetical order:

a)	b)	c)	d)
skill	air	lady	under
mouse	hat	mend	teach
quick	date	leap	telescope
uniform	football	mast	unhappy
pond	what	meat	thunder
tablet	jump	learn	upstairs
case	kangaroo	muddle	

2 This is the heading of a dictionary page:

nab   201   **native**

Which of these words go on that page?

   nap   nasty   natural neat
   name nativity nail

3 Which of the following words go on this page?

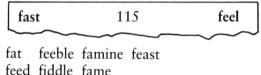

fast   115   **feel**

fat   feeble famine feast
feed fiddle fame

Pronunciation

Use the printed page to work out how to say each of these words:

   giblets   gherkin   gill   gills
   geyser   ghee   ghetto

Meaning

Find two meanings for each of these words:
   gig   ghoul   ghost   gift

Spelling

In these sentences a number of words have been spelled wrongly. Use the dictionary page to correct the spelling.

We had a gastly night last night. Mira was cooking supper. First of all there wasn't any gee, or any other cooking fat. Then she got the chicken out of the fridge and found that Dilip had left the ghiblets in it and it smelled terrible. While she was wondering what to do, there was a loud bang. Dilip rushed in. He looked as if he had seen a gost. He said that the geezer had blown up. All Mira could do was gigle.

Using your own dictionary

1 Find out how to say these words:
   matrix   nitric   covet   psychic
   resound   apiary

2 Find out the meaning of:
   a) the words in question 1
   b) casement   semaphore   nickel
      hessian   aplomb   maw

3 For each of these groups of words use a dictionary to decide which is the correct spelling:
   addres   adress   address
   matress   matriss   mattress
   professor   profesor   proffessor
   weird   weard   wierd
   embarrass   embarras   embarass
   concious   consious   conscious
   sieze   seeze   seize
   exercise   excercise   excercize

Words: spelling

Vowels and consonants

Vowels:

a e i o u

Consonants:

b c d f g h j k l m n p q r s t v w x y z

If V = vowel and C = consonant, think of some words that fit these spelling patterns:

1 CVC   (eg hat)
2 CVCV   (eg rope)
3 CVVC   (eg beat)
4 CVCC   (eg back)
5 CVCVC   (eg ropes)

Long vowels and short vowels

These words contain *short* vowels:

hit   tap   cut

The pattern is: CVC

These words contain *long* vowels:

tame   hate   lean   beat

The patterns are: CVCe
                  CVVC

Make a list of all the words you can think of that fit these three patterns:

CVC
CVCe
CVVC

Adding **ing** and **ed**

The rule:

	+ed	+ing
CVC	CVC C ed	CVC C ing
hop	hopped	hopping
CVCe	CVCe ed	CVCe ing
hope	hoped	hoping
CVVC	CVVC ed	CVVC ing
heap	heaped	heaping

Adding **ly**

The rule:

1 *Most words*

   [   ]ly   quick → quickly

2 Words that end in **l**

   [l]ly   fatal → fatally

3 Words that end in **ll**

   [ll]ly   full → fully

4 Words that end in **y**

   [y]ily   happy → happily

5 Words that end in **le**

   [le]ly   sensible → sensibly

Making plurals

Plural = more than one

1   Most words
    [   ]s   book → books

2   Words that end in **s**
    [s]es   glass → glasses

3   Words that end in **sh** or **ch**
    [sh]es   bush → bushes
    [ch]es   bunch → bunches

4   Most words ending in **f**
    [f]ves   half → halves

5   Most words ending in **fe**
    [fe]ves life → lives

Words ending in **y**

1   Adding **ing**
    [y]ing   fly → flying
                   play → playing

2   Adding other endings
    [y]ies   fly → flies
    [y]ier   funny → funnier
    [y]ily   funny → funnily

3   Words that end **ay ey oy**
    Don't do anything to the **y**:
        tray → trays   boy → boys

Don't get confused

The words in these groups are easily
confused. Show that you know how they are
used, by using them correctly in a sentence.

1   to/too/two
2   hear/here
3   there/their
4   great/grate
5   new/knew
6   loose/lose
7   lead/led
8   right/write
9   now/know
10 where/were

Awkward customers

address	chemist	neighbour
beginning	cough	niece
disappear	cousin	people
embarrass	cupboard	pigeon
exaggerate	electricity	queue
necessary	February	saucer
professional	friend	scissors
success	guard	separate
terrible	headache	special
woollen	height	usually
argument	hospital	vegetable
beautiful	island	Wednesday
business	language	
centre	minute	

Writing sentences

Questions

1 Do you agree with her?
2 How difficult is it to read what she is saying?
3 How many different kinds of punctuation mark would you need to add to make it easier to understand?

Separate sentences

Punctuation makes your writing easier to read and understand. The most important thing it does is to show where one sentence ends and another begins. Each of these passages is made up of one or more sentences. How many sentences are there in each one?

1 Christmas was coming the little log house was almost buried in snow great drifts were banked against the walls and windows, and in the morning when Pa opened the door, there was as wall of snow as high as Laura's head

2 Pa took the shovel and shovelled it away, and then he shovelled a path to the barn, where the horses and cows were snug and warm in their stalls

3 The days were clear and bright Laura and Mary stood on chairs by the window and looked out across the glittering snow at the glittering trees snow was piled all along their their bare, dark branches, and it sparkled in the sunshine

4 Icicles hung from the eves of the house to the snow-banks, great icicles as large at the top as Laura's arm they were like glass and full of sharp lights

Capital letters and full stops

Every sentence begins with a capital letter and ends with a full stop.
Copy out this passage. Divide it into sentences by putting in capital letters and full stops:

ma was very busy all day long, cooking good things for Christmas she baked salt-rising bread and rye'n'Injun bread, and Swedish crackers and a huge pan of beans, with salt pork and molasses she baked vinegar pies and dried-apple pies, and filled a big jar with cookies, and she let Laura and Mary lick the cake spoon one morning she boiled molasses and sugar together until they made a thick syrup, and Pa brought in two pans of clean, white snow from outdoors Laura and Mary each had a pan, and Pa and Ma showed them how to pour the dark syrup in little streams on to the snow they made circles, and curlicues, and squiggledy things, and these hardened at once and were candy Laura and Mary might eat one piece each, but the rest was saved for Christmas Day

Now do the same with this passage:

many, many years ago, a German baron was chasing some robbers on horseback he followed them through the city gate and over the drawbridge as the baron went after them through the gate, the portcullis dropped down, just missing the rider but chopping the horse in two the baron was very quick-thinking a laurel bush grew by the city gates, and the baron took some shoots from the bush and stitched his horse back together again the horse was soon better, and the following Spring the laurel shoots began to grow from then on, the baron could travel in the hottest weather because the leaves of the laurel growing from the horse kept him in the shade

Now your writing

Look through your exercise book. Choose a piece of writing that you have done and read it through. See if you can find places where you should have put full stops and capital letters. Score one point for every time you have missed a full stop or capital letter. Count up the points for that piece of writing.

Now choose another piece and do the same thing.

If you score below five then you are quite an accurate writer – or a poor checker!

For the teacher

The focus in this book is on presenting a wide range of practical and progressive language activities in as accessible and entertaining a way as possible. The main part of the book is arranged thematically so that topics likely to engage children's interest and imagination are readily available. It also offers a systematic introduction to important language techniques such as narrative, exposition, and the expression of opinion.

Themes

There are eight theme units; they contain the following elements:

Starter   A visual and practical introduction to the theme.

Activities   Reading, writing, listening, and talking deriving from some aspect of the theme. Activities pages open up the theme and also give opportunities for practising particular techniques.

Techniques   Each theme unit contains at least one spread which focuses on a specific language technique:

Storytelling: stories in everyday life	pp 32/33
kinds of story	pp 74/75
working out the plot	pp 104/105
Writing poems: first lines and last lines	p 18
The playground poem	p 19
using simile — The monster poem	pp 90/91
Researching and explaining: facts about school	p 6/7
doing a class survey	p 14
explaining charts	p 15
explaining rules and processes	pp 46/47
Describing: writing about people	pp 28/29
viewpoint	pp 60/61
Expressing opinion:	pp 62/63
Wordbuilding:	pp 94/95

Puzzles   Reading activities, such as cloze and sequencing exercises, word games and other puzzles.

Reading   A longer and more demanding passage, usually prose fiction, but occasionally verse. While we have tried to ensure that all other texts and instructions are at a level that average readers can cope with reasonably easily, the reading pages are deliberately more challenging. Many teachers will wish to introduce this material by reading it to the class. The stories and extracts have been chosen for their variety, imaginative interest, and humour.

Using theme units   We envisage that each two-page spread should normally provide material for two timetable periods. Some will take longer to complete. All activities are clearly signalled and written work is usually preceded by preparatory activities.

Once the 'Starter' has been used, the teacher has a choice of route through the unit. This can be summed up in this diagram:

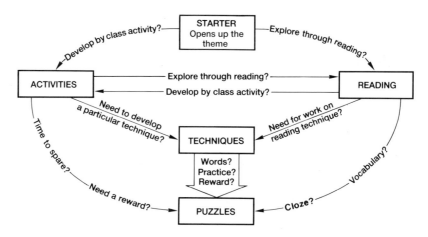

Specials

These are 2-page or 4-page units designed to be used in a different way. There is a strong element of play in them. They present a story or situation usually by means of some kind of evidence — pictures, documents etc. The children have to find their way through this by playing a game, working out a story, or in some other way that challenges their intelligence and imagination. Specials are usually suitable for use either individually or in pairs or small groups. While we hope that children will enjoy them, there is a serious language-teaching purpose behind each of them.

Reference section

The 'nuts and bolts' of writing are presented in reference form with exercises. These are separate from the rest of the book for ease of use, either individually or in class.

Acknowledgements

The publishers wish to thank the following for permission to use photographic material:

Barnaby's Picture Library p. 116 (bottom right); **J. Allan Cash Ltd.** p. 116 (top, middle right and bottom left); **Bruce Coleman Ltd.** p. 63 (top); **Sally & Richard Greenhill** pp. 16 (top left), 30 (middle left, middle, middle right and bottom left), 31 (top, middle left and right and bottom left), 62 (top); **Rob Judges** pp. 16 (bottom and top right), 43, 56 (all), 74 (all), 106 (both), 107 (top), 116 (top left); **Janis Austin/Photo Co-op** p. 30 (top); **Sporting Pictures (UK) Ltd.** p. 31 (middle); **John Twinning** pp. 30 (bottom right), 31 (bottom right), 63 (bottom).

The illustrations are by Andrew Aloof, Judy Brown, Helen Charlton, Alan Curless, Rosamund Fowler, Terry Gabbey, Gerard Gibson, Robina Green, Jonathan Heap, Sue Heap, Tudor Humphries, Marie-Hélène Jeeves, Christyan Jones, Sally Jordan-Kidd, Peter Joyce, Sian Leetham, Karin Littlewood, Alan Marks, Ian Miller, David Murray, Oxford Illustrators, Nicki Palin, R.D.H. Artists, John Ridgway, Amelia Rosato, Susan Scott, Nick Sharratt, Kate Simpson, Maggie Silver, Kendrick Snodin, Gina Toone, Brian Walker, Martin White, Kier Wickenham, Shaun Williams. Cover illustration by Christina Brimage.

The Publishers would like to thank the following for permission to reprint copyright material:

Allan Ahlberg: 'Colin' from *Please Mrs Butler* (Kestrel Books 1983). Copyright © Allan Ahlberg 1983, (pp 64–5). Reprinted by permission of Penguin Books Ltd. **Vivien Alcock:** 'A Fall of Snow' from *Ghostly Companions*. (Associated Book Publishers). **Alan Brownjohn:** 'In this City'. **Dennis Doyle:** 'Four Moons', first published in *Apricot Rhymes* (Common Workshop) and reprinted in *I Like That Stuff* ed. Morag Styles. (Cambridge University Press). **Jane Ferguson:** 'Jacqueline' adapted from *Shivers*. Reprinted by permission of Hippo Books. **Miriam Hodgson:** 'Midas and the Golden Wish' from *A Touch of Gold* (Methuen 1983). Reprinted by permission of Associated Book Publishers Ltd. **Gene Kemp:** 'Caught' from *Gowie Corbie Plays Chicken* (Faber 1979). Reprinted by permission of the publisher. **Laurie Lee:** 'First Day At School' from *Cider With Rosie* (1959). Reprinted by permission of the author and The Hogarth Press Ltd. **Jan Mark:** 'William's Version' from *Nothing to be Afraid Of* (Kestrel Books 1980). Copyright © Jan Mark 1977, 1980, (pp 68–75). Reprinted by permission of Penguin Books Ltd. **Wong May:** 'Only the Moon' from *Seven Poets*. Reprinted by permission of Singapore University Press. **Grace Nichols:** 'I Like to Stay Up' from *I Like that Stuff* edited by Morag Styles. (Cambridge University Press 1984). **Gareth Owen:** 'Shed in Space' from *Song of the City*. Copyright © Gareth Owen 1985. Reprinted by permission of William Collins Sons & Co. Ltd. **Michael Palin:** 'Limericks' reprinted from *Limericks*. (Century Hutchinson Ltd 1985). **R.E. Raspe:** short story from *Singular Travels Campaigns and Adventures of Baron Munchausen*. **Idries Shah:** two short stories from *The Pleasantries of the incredible Mulla Nasrudin*. Reprinted by permission of A.P. Watt Ltd., on behalf of Idries Shah. **John Walsh:** 'The New Boy'. **Laura Ingalls Wilder:** 'Christmas Presents' from *Little House in the Big Woods* (Methuen 1956). Reprinted by permission of Methuen Children's Books. **Kit Wright:** 'Grandad's Dead and I'm Sorry about That', and 'My Party' from *Rabitting On and Other Poems*. Copyright © Kit Wright 1978. Reprinted by permission of William Collins Sons & Co. Ltd.

Every effort has been made to contact copyright owners but sometimes without success. The Publisher will rectify any errors or omissions in future editions if notified.